RECYCLING YOUR ENGLISH

REVISED EDITION

WITH KEY

CLARE WEST

GEORGIAN PRESS

Georgian Press (Jersey) Limited
8 Duhamel Place
St Helier
Jersey JE1 3WF
Channel Islands

First edition published 1993, reprinted 1994
This revised edition first published 1996
Reprinted 1996, 1997, 1998 (twice), 1999, 2001

ISBN 1-873630-10-7 (without key)
ISBN 1-873630-11-5 (with key)

Produced by AMR Limited

Printed in Egypt by International Printing House

CONTENTS

SECTION 3 VOCABULARY

SECTION 4 WRITING

SECTION 5 TESTS

The Key begins on page 113 of the With Key edition.

INTRODUCTION

Who is this book for?

Recycling Your English is for students at upper-intermediate level who wish to improve their general English and/or prepare for the revised Cambridge First Certificate examination (FCE) or the IGCSE in ESL. It can be used to supplement any coursebook at this level, and is suitable for use in the classroom, for homework, or (in the case of the With Key edition) for self-study.

What does Recycling Your English offer?

The book aims to provide:

- coverage of the four main areas of difficulty at upper-intermediate level - grammar, phrasal verbs, vocabulary and writing
- concise, clearly-presented explanations and examples, which are easy to refer to
- extensive practice of each point covered
- a strong element of cumulative recycling, followed up by tests
- a user-friendly, attractive layout, so that the material is accessible and a pleasure to use.

How is the book organised?

It is divided into five distinct sections:

Section 1 GRAMMAR (30 units)

This is the largest section of the book, covering all the major grammatical points at upper-intermediate level. Students are helped to revise and practise what they have learned, and to gain confidence in using grammar correctly.

Section 2 PHRASAL VERBS (12 units)

This section presents fourteen common groups of phrasal verbs and provides extensive practice in varying formats. A useful feature is the attention given to the different possible collocations of phrasal verbs which have more than one meaning.

RECYCLING units are an important element in Sections 1 and 2. They occur after every four or five units and the recycling is cumulative - that is, all previous items are recycled, not just those from the previous group of units.

Section 3 VOCABULARY (12 units)

This section presents and practises vocabulary from twelve key topics which regularly occur in Oral and Composition papers.

Section 4 WRITING (6 units)

The Writing section offers clear guidance on a variety of different writing tasks, with model compositions, notes on style and register, and useful expressions to learn and practise.

Section 5 TESTS (8 units)

The Tests enable students to check their overall progress in assimilating the main points in the book. They also provide valuable extensive practice in dealing with examination-type exercises.

How should Recycling Your English be used?

Teachers using the book as supplementary material should feel free to dip in and out of units and sections as appropriate. However, in Section 1 there is a progression of grammatical items from Units 1 to 30, so students working alone are recommended to work through units chronologically.

Recycling units are also best used in sequence – for example, Unit 5 after Units 1-4.

Each section is independent of the others and can be used at any stage, except for Section 5 TESTS. These should ideally be used at the very end, after all the other sections have been covered, when better results will be obtained. Tests can be done in class, individually, in pairs or small groups, or treated as a class quiz, with teams of students calling out answers, or set as homework.

What changes are there in the Revised Edition?

Recycling Your English has been revised to reflect the altered approach of the revised FCE examination, and to offer practice in as many as possible of the new exercise types. Numerous improvements and additions suggested by frequent users of the book have also been incorporated. Thanks are extended to all the people who offered their comments.

The five sections have been changed as follows:

Section 1 GRAMMAR

This section has been revised and expanded to include units on Conjunctions, Modals, Adjectives and Adverbs, plus a new Recycling unit.

Section 2 PHRASAL VERBS

Two new units have been added, covering phrasal verbs with Set, Stand, Run, See, Give and Break.

Section 3 VOCABULARY

This section now includes units on People and Lifestyles, and Entertainment and the Media.

Section 4 WRITING

This section has been revised and expanded, with more material on Formal and Informal Letters, and Discursive Compositions, and the addition of work on Articles and Reports, and Set Texts.

Section 5 TESTS

This section now contains a wider variety of exercise types, including a greater number of text-based exercises.

It is hoped that teachers and students who have used **Recycling Your English** in the past will consider this an improved version and that others will enjoy using it for the first time.

Present Simple and Present Continuous

The Present Simple is used to talk about

a actions done regularly or frequently, often with adverbs like **never, seldom, occasionally, sometimes, often, usually** and **always**:

- *David usually plays football on Saturday.* - *What do you do in the evenings?*

b facts that are always or usually true:

- *Elephants don't eat meat.* - *She comes from Cairo.*

The Present Continuous is used to talk about things that are happening now, at the moment of speaking, often with adverbs like **now, at the moment, at present, today, this week,** etc:

- *Elena is writing a letter at the moment. She's writing to Maria.*

A Complete the sentences, using the Present Simple or the Present Continuous.

1 He always _____ chocolate after lunch. (eat)
2 I can't come. I _____ my mother. (help)
3 They _____ hard enough at present. (not / study)
4 They often _____ coffee in the evenings. (drink)
5 Clara occasionally _____ to the theatre. (go)
6 Yukiko _____ a bath now. (have)
7 We _____ a cake at the moment. (make)
8 I never _____ cigarettes. (smoke)
9 She _____ her hair twice a week. (wash)
10 Lisa _____ her sister's car today. (drive)
11 The Amazon _____ into the Atlantic. (flow)
12 Many birds _____ south for the winter. (fly)

B Write full sentences using the information given. EXAMPLE: You / enjoy / the party? *Are you enjoying the party?*

1 You / speak / Greek? _____
2 Bill / know / Mr Jameson? _____
3 We / not live / in a large house. _____
4 Alexander / not go / to the beach very often. _____
5 I / have to / attend the ceremony? _____
6 Jane / watch / television at the moment? _____
7 Costas / not work / in a bank. _____
8 The children / not listen / to their mother now. _____
9 Theo / live / in New York? _____
10 William / study / at the moment? _____
11 Where / you / usually spend / your holidays? _____
12 I / not earn much money at present. _____

The following verbs do **not** normally take the **Continuous** form:
- *believe, belong, contain, dislike, doubt, hate, impress, know, like, love, mean, need, owe, own, prefer, resemble, seem, suppose, surprise, understand, want, wish*

The following verbs can be used in the **Simple or Continuous** form but with different meanings:
- *appear, feel, see, smell, taste, think*

C Complete the sentences, using the correct present tense of the verbs in brackets.

1 A famous actress _____ in a play at the local theatre. (appear)
2 I'm sure she _____ tea to coffee. (prefer)
3 His story _____ to be true. (appear)
4 George _____ of visiting Turkey this summer. (think)
5 Rupert says the book _____ to him. (belong)
6 The director _____ that would be a mistake. (believe)
7 Louisa _____ having supper late. (hate)
8 This pasta _____ simply delicious. (taste)
9 There _____ to be something wrong with the photocopier. (seem)
10 *Now* I _____ what the teacher _____ . (understand, mean)
11 You'd better not drink that milk. It _____ bad. (smell)
12 Frank _____ me a lot of money! (owe)

D Complete the sentences, using the correct present tense of the verbs in brackets.

1 He usually _____ very hard, but he _____ at all today because it's a holiday. (work, not / work)
2 Look! That man _____ out of the bank! And he _____ a large bag full of money! (run, carry)
3 I don't mind babysitting for you. Your baby never _____. (cry)
4 Every time he _____ a photo, his hand _____, and his photos never _____ good. (take, shake, look)
5 'Can you come out for a drink with us later?' 'Sorry, I _____ Liza with her work, and it'll take us hours to finish it.' (help)
6 She usually _____ a BMW, but today she _____ her husband's Volvo. (drive)
7 'Where do you live?' 'Normally I _____ in Paris with my parents, but at the moment I _____ in London, so I _____ with an English family.' (live, study, live)
8 I know you _____ because you _____ out of the window! (not / listen, look)
9 Julia _____ five languages fluently, and at the moment she _____ as a translator. (speak, work)
10 I _____ three pullovers in winter because I always _____ cold. (wear, feel)
11 Wood _____ on water. (float)
12 'Why _____ you _____?' 'Because nobody _____ me, that's why!' (cry, love)

Past Simple and Present Perfect
(Simple and Continuous)

The Past Simple is used to talk about completed actions at a particular point in the past, often with dates or times and words like **yesterday**, **last** and **ago**:

• *Kurt went to Canada in 1991.* • *I didn't see you yesterday. Where were you?*

The Present Perfect is used to talk about

a recent actions or events when no fixed time is given (e.g. news reports), often with words like **just**, **recently** and **lately**:

  • *A volcano has erupted in Japan.* • *I've just seen your mother in the street.*

b actions which have a result in the present:

  • *What's wrong? Have you lost your keys?*

c actions in a period of time which is not yet finished, and experiences in someone's life so far, often with **yet**, **so far**, **ever**, **for** and **since**:

  • *I haven't had any letters this week.* (Compare: *I had five letters last week.*)
  • *She's visited New York five times.* (in her life so far)
  • *Have you ever been to Greece?*

The Present Perfect Continuous is used to talk about actions which started in the past and are still happening, or which have recently stopped but have a result in the present:

  • *I've been waiting here for ten minutes.*
  • *Your eyes are red. You haven't been crying, have you?*

A Complete the sentences, using the Past Simple, the Present Perfect or the Present Perfect Continuous, and the words in brackets.
Remember — many verbs have irregular forms: check on page 112.

1 Rafael _____ shopping for me yesterday. (go)

2 Sandra _____ her brother £200 so far. (lend)

3 The policeman _____ ten minutes ago. (drive away)

4 The biscuit factory _____ last year. (close down)

5 She's very red. I think she _____ in the sun. (lie)

6 Raschid _____ his driving test. (just / pass)

7 Karen _____ Italian for three years now and is still studying. (study)

8 The headmaster _____ to the school in 1985. (come)

9 Jack _____ to get a job for six months, but is still unemployed. (try)

10 The teacher _____ him to be quiet. (already / tell)

11 Tim _____ many photos yet. (not / take)

12 Oh no! I _____ my purse at home. (leave)

13 They _____ in love with each other at first sight. (fall)

14 I don't want a bath, thanks. I _____ a shower. (just / have)

15 I'm sorry, I _____ your name. What did you say it was? (forget)

B Write full sentences using the information given. EXAMPLE: He / go / to the class last week? *Did he go to the class last week?*

1 When / you / last go / to Spain?
2 You / ever speak / to a film star?
3 You / spend / a lot of money last month?
4 I / not say / anything up to now.
5 Laura / not have / a holiday so far this year.
6 You / see / any good films lately?
7 You / ever / be / to Japan?
8 Helmut / write / to you yet?
9 The boys / finish / their homework yesterday?
10 Rolf / not buy / the leather jacket last week.

C Complete the sentences with *for* or *since*.
Remember – *since* refers to a fixed point in time; *for* refers to a period of time and can be used with different tenses.

1 I haven't seen him _____ ages.
2 Maria hasn't played tennis _____ last summer.
3 Bob and I have been friends _____ years.
4 _____ his birthday, Peter has been behaving rather strangely.
5 Mr Brown worked in New York _____ ten weeks.
6 They waited outside the cinema _____ half an hour.
7 Peter has been in this country _____ January 27th 1990.
8 We lived in Paris _____ a long time before moving to Brussels.
9 I've been waiting for the doctor _____ 4.30.
10 I'm sorry I haven't written _____ so long.

D Complete the passage, using the correct tense of the verbs in brackets.

Good evening. This is the nine o'clock news. At least three people 1) _____ (die) in a serious accident on a narrow road in the north–west Highlands. A minibus carrying eight businessmen 2) _____ (crash) into a tourist coach just after 11 o'clock this morning. There 3) _____ (be) thick fog at the time. A local farmer 4) _____ (see) the crash and 5) _____ (alert) the emergency services, who 6) _____ (rush) to the scene. They 7) _____ (work) there for the last two hours, and they 8) _____ (just / manage) to free the last survivor. A helicopter 9) _____ (already / take) the most seriously injured to hospital in Glasgow. The police 10) _____ (not / release) any names yet.

In the Crown Court a judge 11) _____ (sentence) a doctor to two years in prison for causing the death of a patient. Dr Rita Daniels 12) _____ (tell) the court two days ago that she 13) _____ (stop) her treatment of 79-year-old Norman Smith because he was suffering from an incurable blood disease and she 14) _____ (want) to save him from any more pain. The jury 15) _____ (find) her guilty of unlawful killing, but Dr Daniels' lawyer 16) _____ (ask) for her to be set free. However, when the trial came to an end yesterday, the judge 17) _____ (decide) she must be punished, and 18) _____ (send) her to prison.

UNIT 3

Past Simple and Past Continuous

> **The Past Continuous** is used to talk about continuous actions which are interrupted by a Past Simple action:
>
> - *I was having my breakfast when the police arrived.*
>
> It is also used for descriptions and to set the scene when telling a story:
>
> - *It was raining hard as I walked down the road.*

A Complete the sentences, setting the scene for a story.

1 It _____ foggier as we drove further into the forest. (get)
2 The sun _____ when I woke up. (shine)
3 It _____ so hard that we decided to stay at home. (snow)
4 Alex _____ a newspaper in the library. (read)
5 The birds _____ in the early morning sunshine. (sing)

B Complete the sentences, using the Past Simple and the Past Continuous.

1 I _____ television when the phone _____. (watch, ring)
2 Keith _____ a bath when the detective _____. (have, arrive)
3 Alberto _____ a leg when he _____. (break, ski)
4 Last night Lydia _____ to the radio when she _____ a strange noise downstairs. (listen, hear)
5 Jim _____ out of the tree while he _____ it. (fall, climb)
6 We _____ Kate first aid when the ambulance _____. (give, arrive)
7 While I _____ , I _____ an old man lying on the ground. (wait, notice)
8 Rachel _____ not to go out, because it _____. (decide, rain)
9 The thief _____ my purse while I _____ at the shop window. (steal, look)
10 The other day Heidi _____ the road when suddenly a car _____ into a lamp-post in front of her. (cross, crash)

C Look at these examples:
What were you doing when the police arrived? I was having my breakfast. What did you do when the police arrived? I answered their questions.
Now choose the best answer (A-F) for each question.

1 What were you doing before you watched the film? ___
2 What did you do when you saw the burglar? ___
3 What was he doing during the lesson? ___
4 What were they doing at the time of the robbery? ___
5 What did they do when the fire alarm rang? ___
6 What did he do when the policeman arrived? ___

A I rang the police.	D They rushed outside.
B I was watching the news.	E He climbed out of the window.
C They were eating in a restaurant.	F He was listening to the teacher.

Past Simple and Past Perfect

The Past Perfect is used to show that a completed action happened **before** something else in the past: • *I telephoned Jane at 4.30, but she had already left the office.*

But if two past actions are close in time, or closely connected, the Past Perfect is not usually used: • *When he arrived at the hotel, he asked for a room.*

The Past Perfect Continuous is used to show that there had been continuous or repeated action before something else in the past:

• *I was very angry when the bus finally came, because I'd been waiting a long time for it.*

A Complete the sentences, using the correct past tense of the verb in brackets.
Remember – some verbs do not take the continuous form.

1 Susan no longer owned a bike. She _____ it. (sell)
2 Mary looked very pale when she arrived for the exam. She _____ too hard. (study)
3 The boy's knee was bleeding when he arrived home. He _____. (fall over)
4 I invited Silvia to the party but she couldn't come. She _____ to go somewhere else. (arrange)
5 Chris bought a loaf of bread and took it home, but Maria _____ one. (already / buy)
6 I was annoyed when someone bought those shoes in the shop window, because I _____ for them. (save up)
7 The guide offered us tickets for a musical, but Elena _____ it. (already / see)
8 I knew I recognized the town square. I _____ there before. (be)

B Look at these examples:
Before Simon went to the hotel, he bought some books. After he had bought some books, he went to the hotel. (or: After buying some books)
Now complete the sentences, using the correct past tense of the verbs in brackets.

1 After Richard _____ work, he _____ home. (finish, go)
2 By the time the firemen _____, the fire _____. (arrive, already / go out)
3 Before she _____ the school, Celia _____ goodbye to all her friends. (leave, say)
4 After _____ his homework, Joe _____ . (do, go out)
5 When Yuko _____ home, she _____ her friend at once. (reach, phone)
6 After she _____ all the way home, Linda _____ quite exhausted. (run, feel)

C Correct the sentences if necessary. Tick any which are already correct.

1 Before Dora had done the shopping, she visited her neighbour.
2 When the programme finished, Ali switched the television off.
3 After buying their tickets, the two businessmen caught the train.
4 When Guy passed the exam, his father had been buying him a car.
5 It's a lovely fire, isn't it? I'd only put a match to it a few minutes ago.
6 We watered the garden after planting the seeds.
7 I'm rather tired because I had been running to get here on time.

Recycling

A Choose the correct word or phrase to complete each sentence. Write the letter in the space.

1 Water _____ at 100 degrees Celsius.

a) boiling   b) boils   c) is boiling   d) boil

2 Bettina usually _____ television in the evening.

a) watches   b) watching   c) watch   d) has watched

3 Rosemary _____ to agree with us now.

a) is appearing   b) appear   c) appeared   d) appears

4 Look! That man _____ your bike!

a) is stealing   b) steals   c) stealing   d) stolen

5 I'm sorry I _____ to do my homework yesterday.

a) am forgetting   b) have forgotten   c) forgot   d) forget

6 We _____ any interesting films lately.

a) didn't see   b) haven't seen   c) saw   d) have seen

7 Eric _____ a flat yet, so he's still living with his parents.

a) found   b) didn't find   c) is finding   d) hasn't found

8 They _____ running their own company in 1980.

a) started   b) have started   c) are starting   d) start

9 She's a law student and she _____ for four years now.

a) studied   b) is studying   c) has been studying   d) did study

10 I think I _____ my door key. I can't find it anywhere.

a) lost   b) have lost   c) am losing   d) will lose

11 The film _____ when we arrived at the cinema.

a) has begun   b) begun   c) had begun   d) begins

12 I wasn't thirsty because I _____ some milk.

a) drunk   b) have just drunk   c) just drank   d) had just drunk

13 When the match was over, the spectators _____ home.

a) went   b) had gone   c) were going   d) have gone

14 After having a bath, he _____ his supper.

a) had eaten   b) ate   c) has eaten   d) was eating

15 The phone _____ suddenly while Joanne was doing the housework.

a) rang   b) was ringing   c) had rung   d) is ringing

16 It _____ as we drove slowly along the road.

a) has snowed   b) had snowed   c) was snowing   d) is snowing

17 Mrs Edwards _____ history for 35 years, and is retiring soon.

a) teaches   b) is teaching   c) taught   d) has been teaching

18 Did you see John yesterday? He _____ a very old pair of jeans.

a) wears   b) didn't wear   c) was wearing   d) wore

19 Victoria _____ for half an hour when the doctor finally arrived.

a) has been waiting   b) had been waiting   c) was waiting
d) has waited

20 Anita _____ very hard at the moment.

a) is studying   b) studies   c) studied   d) has studied

B Complete the second sentence so that it has a similar meaning to the first one. Use between two and five words, including the word given. Do not change the word given.

1 I last went shopping two months ago.   BEEN

I _____ two months.

2 Our last holiday was in Greece.   TO

We _____ our last holiday.

3 I've been here for two hours, and I'm still waiting.   WAITING

I _____ two hours.

4 I haven't seen him for ages.   SINCE

It's _____ seen him.

5 The burglar escaped before the police arrived.   HAD

When the police _____ escaped.

6 Fred fell off a ladder while painting a wall.   WAS

While _____, he fell off a ladder.

7 The workmen finished, and then Mr Jenkins came home.   WHEN

The workmen _____ came home.

8 Evie made an appointment, and went to see the doctor.   MAKING

Evie went to _____ an appointment.

9 First he booked the hall, and then he invited everybody.   BEFORE

He booked the hall _____ everybody.

10 I walked home in heavy rain.   AS

It _____ I walked home.

C Some of the lines in this letter are correct, and others have a word which should not be there. Tick any lines which are correct. Write down any words which should not be there.

Dear Roberto,

    Thank you for your letter which has arrived last week. I'm   ☐ 1
sorry I haven't written to you for two months ago. I've been so   ☐ 2
busy at college, I simply haven't had time. Don't be angry with   ☐ 3
me!

    Do you like the English family you are been staying with?   ☐ 4
Have you being started your new English course yet? Do your   ☐ 5
teachers not give you a lot of homework? I hope not, but I expect   ☐ 6
they do. Anyway, don't be forget, I can help you with it if it's   ☐ 7
difficult! And what about London? Have you already been on the   ☐ 8
Underground yet?

    You'll never guess what was happened to me last week. It was   ☐ 9
Tuesday morning, and I was walking along the road near my   ☐ 10
house, when suddenly two men with guns have rushed out of the   ☐ 11
bank! I went to the nearest phone box and rang to the police.   ☐ 12
Unfortunately, by the time they were arrived (it seemed to take   ☐ 13
them a very long time), the bank robbers had escaped. It was all   ☐ 14
very exciting, anyway! I think there'll be a picture of me in the   ☐ 15
local paper! Fame at last!

    Now it's your turn to write! Have fun!

    Best wishes,

    Thomas

Conditionals

> **The First Conditional** is used for a possible future action which depends on another action:
>
> - *If Ali works hard, he'll pass the exam.*
> - *We'll get there on time if we leave now.*
>
> **The Zero Conditional** is used for a situation which is always true:
>
> - *If water is colder than O° Celsius, it freezes.*
>
> **Remember** – **unless** means **if not**. Do not use **will** after **if**.
>
> **The Second Conditional** is used for an imaginary situation, where the meaning is in the present:
>
> - *If I had more money, I would (I'd) buy a car.*
>   (I haven't got enough money at the moment.)
>
> It can also be used for a remote possibility in the future:
> - *If I won the competition, I'd go on a world cruise.*
> and for giving advice:
> - *If I were you, I'd stay at home.* (**were** is usually preferred to **was** in this case)

A Write First or Zero Conditional sentences.

1 If / the sun / shine / we / go / for a walk.
2 People / can / not / ski / in the Alps / if / there / be / no snow.
3 Unless Isabelle / run / she / not catch / the bus.
4 You / be able to / drive my car / if you / pass / your driving test.
5 Unless you / go / to bed early / you / be / tired tomorrow.
6 Ice always / melt / if the air temperature / be / warm enough.
7 I / not / sign / the contract / unless / you / agree / to it.
8 If you / have / time / you / be able to / visit the exhibition.

B Complete the second sentence so that it has a similar meaning to the first one. Use between two and five words, including the word given. Do not change the word given.

1 I might win £1000, and then I'd travel to Australia.   IF
  I'd travel to Australia _____ £1000.
2 Our heating isn't working and I feel cold.   I
  If our heating were_____ so cold.
3 Hans should give up smoking to improve his health.   WOULD
  If Hans _____ improve his health.
4 Maybe I could go to Arizona and visit Joe.   WENT
  If I _____ visit Joe.
5 I think you should revise for the exam.   YOU
  If I _____ for the exam.
6 I don't speak Spanish well enough to work in Mexico.   BETTER
  If I _____ work in Mexico.

The **Third Conditional** is used for an imaginary situation referring to a past action:

- *If he hadn't stolen the money, he wouldn't have gone to prison.*
  (But he stole the money, so he went to prison.)

Notice this 'mixed Conditional' sentence:

- *If he hadn't stolen the money, he wouldn't be in prison now.*
  (But he stole the money, so he's in prison now.)

When can be used instead of **if**, but only if it is certain that something will happen:

- *When he arrives, I'll thank him.* (I know he's going to arrive.)

Do not use **will** after **when, after, before, as soon as, until, till** and **while**. When they are used to refer to a real future action, they take the same structure as the First Conditional. The **Present Perfect** can sometimes be used after them:

- *I'll wait here until the doctor arrives/has arrived.*

C Write Third Conditional sentences, using the verbs in brackets.

1 He _____ an accident if he _____ more carefully. (not / have, drive)

2 If Linda _____ her the money, Sophie _____ the stereo system. (not / lend, not / buy)

3 I _____ him a birthday card if someone _____ me. (send, remind)

4 If you _____ better last night, you _____ so tired now. (sleep, not / be)

5 Ramon _____ the train if he _____ to the station on time. (catch, get)

D Join each pair of sentences to make one sentence, using *when, after, before, as soon as, until,* or *while*. EXAMPLE: They will arrive soon. I want to finish this work first. *I want to finish this work before they arrive.*

1 You'll leave Athens soon. You must visit the Parthenon first.

2 He'll come home. He'll get his supper then.

3 You'll be on holiday. I'll water your plants for you.

4 The programme will finish soon. I'll switch off the television immediately.

5 I'll go on applying for jobs. One day I'll get one.

6 I'll have a shower. Then I'll cook the dinner.

E Complete the second sentence so that it has a similar meaning to the first one. Use between two and five words, including the word given. Do not change the word given.

1 You can't make a cake without flour.   HAVE
Unless you _____ make a cake.

2 We haven't got any money so we can't have a snack.   SOME
If we _____ have a snack.

3 I hope the weather will clear up. Then I'll be able to go out.   BETTER
If the weather _____ able to go out.

4 I feel rather sick because I ate too much last night.   SO
If I _____ last night, I wouldn't feel so sick now.

5 I didn't notice him. That's why I didn't say hello.   WOULD
If I _____ have said hello.

6 If nobody rings the police, he'll get away with the money.   UNLESS
He'll get away with the money _____ police.

Passives

> **The passive** is used to describe an action when it is not so important who or what did the action, or when we do not know:
>
> - *Mike's car was damaged in an accident.*
>   (= Someone damaged Mike's car in an accident.)
>
> It is often used to describe scientific processes:
>
> - *The water is filtered before it is mixed with the chemicals.*
>
> The object of an active sentence becomes the subject of a passive one; the verb **be** is used in the same tense, with the past participle of the relevant verb. **By** is only used if a name, or a noun giving necessary information, is included:
>
> - *The guide showed him round.* (active)   *He was shown round by the guide.* (passive)
>
> Note the very common passive: • *She was born in Zurich.*

A Turn these sentences from active to passive.
Remember – only include *by* plus a noun or pronoun if this information is necessary.

1 They hold the prizegiving in the hall every year.
2 A storm has brought down all the power cables.
3 Last year the government raised the price of gas.
4 They made all the arrangements for the President's visit.
5 Had he invited her before last weekend?
6 She's renewing her passport next week.
7 The authorities are building blocks of flats all over the town.
8 The police have not investigated the theft yet.
9 The two businessmen signed the contract.
10 They will collect the bottles for recycling.
11 The Mayor is opening the new theatre on Saturday.
12 They were milking the cows when I arrived at the farm.

B Verbs which take the infinitive (e.g. *will, going to*) can be followed by a passive infinitive: *I can do it.* (active) *It can be done.* (passive)
Remember – phrasal verbs or verbs with prepositions must keep their prepositions: *That rubbish will have to be taken away.*
Complete the sentences, using the correct form of the verb in brackets.

1 All the smugglers will _____ by tomorrow. (arrest)
2 The matter should _____ at our next meeting. (bring up)
3 Our electricity bill ought to _____ next week. (pay)
4 It cannot _____ that the company is in financial trouble. (deny)
5 His house is going to _____ next week. (paint)
6 An extension to the sports centre could _____ if necessary. (build)
7 All your homework should _____ by tomorrow. (do)
8 Cars may _____ here free of charge. (park)
9 Since our arrival, we _____ very well. (look after)
10 That carpet will have to _____ again. (clean)
11 The doctor must _____ as soon as possible. (send for)
12 Many more workers will soon _____ by the factory manager. (take on)

C When a sentence has two objects (direct and indirect), the indirect object usually becomes the subject in a passive sentence:
We gave him a book. (active)   *He was given a book.* (passive)
Decide which of the following pairs of sentences is more acceptable.

1a) She was awarded a degree in economics.
  b) A degree in economics was awarded to her.

2a) A farewell present will be given to the actress.
  b) The actress will be given a farewell present.

3a) A bike has been promised to me for my birthday.
  b) I have been promised a bike for my birthday.

4a) A difficult question was asked to Hassan.
  b) Hassan was asked a difficult question.

5a) They are being shown the new flat.
  b) The new flat is being shown to them.

6a) A box of chocolates was given to Miho by Pat.
  b) Miho was given a box of chocolates by Pat.

7a) Why wasn't the truth told to me?
  b) Why wasn't I told the truth?

8a) I was handed £4 change by the assistant.
  b) £4 change was handed to me by the assistant.

9a) The workers might be given a pay rise.
  b) A pay rise might be given to the workers.

10a) A beautiful painting was shown to me by the guide.
   b) I was shown a beautiful painting by the guide.

D Look at this passive – *ing* form: *I remember being taken to the zoo as a child.* Now complete the sentences, using the passive.

1 I don't mind / be / give / presents!
2 Charlotte hates / be / treat / like a baby.
3 He's used to / his English / be / correct.
4 I don't enjoy / be / make / to do the washing-up.
5 I can't stand / be / ignore.
6 He doesn't remember / be / punish / at school.
7 I'm looking forward to / be / send / abroad by my company.
8 My dog simply loves / be / take / for a walk.
9 You'll never forget / be / teach / by your very first teacher.
10 Yesterday I spent two hours / be / show / how to use the new computer.

E Put the words into the correct order to make passive sentences.

1 Fortnight the before sent the were a wedding invitations.
2 Passport the officials be my I stamped hope will by airport.
3 Week number at delivered newspapers were no last 25.
4 Cannot without help be problem the the solved government's.
5 Pitch the flooded to cancelled match the had be rain when.
6 The will results published the in journals scientific of experiments leading be.
7 Presented he large party his at retirement was a with cheque.
8 Travel be must June by arrangements completed all 17th.

Supposition

Say, **think**, **believe**, **know**, **understand**, **consider**, **report** and **suppose** can be used with either of two passive constructions to show that something is supposed to be true:

- *Pepe is said to be very rich.* • *It is said that Pepe is very rich.* (present)
- *Pepe is thought to have robbed a bank.* • *It is thought that Pepe (has) robbed a bank.* (past)

A Complete the second sentence so that it has a similar meaning to the first one. Use between two and five words, including the word given. Do not change the word given.

1 It is reported that a train has crashed in Berlin.   HAVE
  A train _____ crashed in Berlin.

2 The Prime Minister is thought to be considering the plan.   THAT
  It is thought _____ considering the plan.

3 It is believed that priceless jewels have been stolen.   TO
  Priceless jewels _____ stolen.

4 Football is considered to be the world's most popular sport.   IS
  It is considered _____ the world's most popular sport.

5 Diamonds are said to be a girl's best friend.   ARE
  It is _____ a girl's best friend.

6 It is known that Roland inherited a lot of money.   TO
  Roland _____ inherited a lot of money.

7 It is understood that the President is out of the country.   BE
  The President _____ out of the country.

8 It is supposed that too much chocolate is bad for you.   SUPPOSED
  Too much chocolate _____ bad for you.

B Turn these sentences from active to passive.
Remember – only include *by* plus a noun or pronoun if this information is necessary.

1 People say we'll run out of oil one day.

2 The police reported that no witnesses had come forward to give statements.

3 Everybody considers this a wonderful opportunity for young people.

4 Most people believe the solution to the mystery will never be discovered.

5 His lawyer considers him guilty.

6 People think the local cinema will close down soon.

7 Everybody in the area knows that the Robinson family moved away last week.

8 Doctors say we should eat more fruit and vegetables.

9 Our man in Paris reports that prices are rising there.

10 I understand that Stuart won't be in the team this season.

11 The forecasters think the weather will improve next week.

12 Most people know that the British Isles were once part of the European land mass.

Question Tags

> **Question tags** are short questions at the end of a sentence, either requesting information (when the voice goes up) or inviting agreement (when the voice goes down). Positive tags are normally used with negative sentences, and negative tags with positive sentences:
>
> - *You don't live here, do you?* • *John enjoyed the meal, didn't he?*
>
> As well as **do** and **did** (with Present and Past Simple), other auxiliary verbs are used in question tags:
>
> - *He isn't very friendly, is he?* • *I can park here, can't I?*
> - *You've eaten all the cake, haven't you?*
>
> The question tag after an imperative is **will you**, and after **Let's** it is **shall we**:
>
> - *Don't forget to ring, will you?* • *Let's pay the bill, shall we?*
>
> Be careful with:
>
> - *She'd rather stay at home, wouldn't she?*
> - *You'd better have a rest, hadn't you?* • *I'm late, aren't I?*

A Complete the sentences, using the correct question tag.

1 It's a lovely day, _____?
2 Tom drives very fast, _____?
3 You haven't got my book in your bag, _____?
4 He won't mind helping, _____?
5 She wrote the poem herself, _____?
6 That was exciting, _____?
7 We aren't there yet, _____?
8 You couldn't lend me £5, _____?
9 Sarah isn't still waiting, _____?
10 You don't like him, _____?
11 We can stay at Fred's house, _____?
12 I don't think he's ever been there, _____?

B Now complete these sentences with question tags.

1 He'd rather go to the theatre, _____?
2 Get a loaf of bread for me, _____?
3 They'd better attend the meeting, _____?
4 I'm right, _____?
5 Let's go for a swim, _____?
6 Open the window, _____?
7 You'd rather have a salad, _____?
8 Let's play football, _____?
9 They hadn't been there before, _____?
10 She had to complain to the manager, _____?

Recycling

A Choose the correct word or phrase to complete each sentence. Write the letter in the space.

1 We'll give him the message as soon as he _____ .
 a) phones   b) will phone   c) will have phoned   d) is phoning

2 Sam's on his way, so make him a coffee _____ he arrives.
 a) if   b) until   c) while   d) when

3 If I _____ you, I'd apply for that job.
 a) had been   b) were   c) am   d) weren't

4 You'd better go to bed early, _____ ?
 a) hadn't you   b) didn't you   c) wouldn't you   d) don't you

5 If I _____ ill, I wouldn't have been absent from school.
 a) hadn't been   b) weren't   c) had been   d) would have been

6 Unless you _____ harder, you won't succeed.
 a) will try   b) try   c) are trying   d) have tried

7 I'll just have to wait at the stop _____ the bus turns up.
 a) before   b) after   c) while   d) until

8 This broken cup cannot _____ .
 a) repair   b) to be repaired   c) be repaired   d) repairing

9 Let's ask him a question, _____ ?
 a) will we   b) shall we   c) won't we   d) don't we

10 The man is thought _____ .
 a) to have died   b) to dying   c) have died   d) to die

11 You are _____ to clean the bathroom.
 a) declared   b) imagined   c) supposed   d) spoken

12 She'd rather watch television, _____ ?
 a) didn't she   b) hadn't she   c) had she   d) wouldn't she

13 No mistakes _____ made.
 a) has been   b) have been   c) is   d) to be

14 I don't mind _____ waiting for a few minutes.
 a) to be kept   b) keeping   c) being kept   d) being

15 It is _____ that Omar moved to Bahrain.
 a) known   b) told   c) knowing   d) supposing

16 We can't ski unless _____ snow on the slopes.
 a) it is   b) there will be   c) it   d) there is

17 Sheila is understood _____ won the first prize.
 a) having   b) to having   c) to has   d) to have

18 The new motorway _____ and built last year.
 a) planned   b) was planned   c) was planning   d) had planned

19 Get me some stamps, _____ ?
 a) have you   b) do you   c) will you   d) haven't you

20 The photos _____ in a London studio last week.
 a) were taken   b) have taken   c) was taken   d) have been taken

B Complete the second sentence so that it has a similar meaning to the first one. Use between two and five words, including the word given. Do not change the word given.

1 She was still baking the bread in the kitchen.   BAKED
The bread _____ in the kitchen.

2 He'll graduate soon. Then he'll find a job.   WHEN
He'll find a job _____.

3 How long have they been doing this exercise?   START
When _____ this exercise?

4 She could not type the report in time.   BE
The report _____ in time.

5 I haven't done any gardening for three months.   WAS
The last time I _____ three months ago.

6 Zoë is in hospital because she broke her leg.   HADN'T
If Zoë _____, she wouldn't be in hospital now.

7 The college has awarded her a diploma.   BEEN
She _____ a diploma.

8 We'll only be able to come if we can get some time off.   UNLESS
We won't be able to come _____ some time off.

C Some of the lines in this letter are correct, and others have a word which should not be there. Tick any lines which are correct. Write down any words which should not be there.

Dear Roberto,

Thank you for your letter. I am glad to hear you are enjoying [1]
well. When I will have some free time, perhaps I'll come to London [2]
to see you, and then we can go out for a meal together somewhere. [3]

I've just got back from a trip to Lisbon. My father has just been [4]
opened a big new factory in Portugal, and he had wanted me to [5]
help him with marketing. Lisbon is often said to be a very [6]
beautiful city, but I didn't have the chance to see much of it! Dad [7]
always makes me work hard! We had went to lots of business [8]
meetings, and I met all the staff. It would have been some more [9]
useful if I did had learnt Portuguese instead of French at school! [10]
But luckily they all are speak very good English. In fact, Dad's [11]
partner was invited me to lunch, and promised to teach me [12]
Portuguese, so maybe I'll be accept his offer next time. You don't [13]
speak Portuguese, do you?

On my way home, the plane was being delayed for four hours, [14]
because of fog, I think. And poor Samantha was been waiting at [15]
the airport all that time for me! It must be true love! [16]

Keep in touch.

Best wishes,

Thomas

Reported Speech

> **Reported Speech** is used to report to a third person what someone else said. To change sentences from Direct Speech to Reported Speech, the pronoun, tense and time phrase may all be changed:
>
> • *'I'm working tonight,' Daniel said.* (Direct)
>   *Daniel said (that) he was working that night.* (Reported)
>
> In Reported Speech using 2nd and 3rd Conditional sentences, the tenses are not changed:
>
> • *'If you went to bed earlier, you wouldn't feel so tired in the morning,' said his mother.*
>   *His mother told him that if he went to bed earlier, he wouldn't feel so tired in the morning.*

A Turn these sentences into Reported Speech. Choose from these time phrases where necessary: *that morning, the day before, the following week, the following day, that day.*

1 'I'm going to London next week,' said Elisa.

2 'He speaks very good German,' said the teacher.

3 'I come from Izmir,' said Philip's wife.

4 'He broke out of prison yesterday,' said the policewoman.

5 'I've just passed my driving test,' said Ursula.

6 'They're building a museum in the main square,' said the guide.

7 'I'll help Joe as much as I can,' said Mrs Hall.

8 'I work eight hours a day, except when the children are on holiday,' said Maria.

9 'I haven't seen Bridget for ages,' said Michael.

10 'I think I forgot to lock the front door this morning,' said Rosemary.

B Complete the sentences, using the correct tense of the verbs in brackets.

1 She said that if he _____ soon, she _____ him the present. (come, give)

2 He said he _____ at Jill if he _____ how unhappy she was. (not / laugh, know)

3 Mrs Johnson said she _____ me in future if she _____. (help, can)

4 The manager told her that unless she _____ the bill immediately, he _____ the police. (pay, call)

5 He said he _____ if he _____ more careful last time. (not / fall, be)

6 Foster said that he _____ famous if he _____ the race at the next Olympics. (be, win)

7 She said that she _____ the accident if she _____ ill at the time. (not / have, not / be)

8 I told him that he _____ his last job if he _____ harder. (not / lose, work)

C These sentences use more interesting reporting verbs than *say* or *tell*. Note the verbs and which structures follow them.
Turn the sentences into Direct Speech.
EXAMPLE: Susan offered to open the window.
'Shall I open the window?' said/asked Susan.

1 Mark invited Sam to the cinema.
2 Pierre suggested that they should all go to the beach.
3 Zoraya advised her to tell the truth.
4 Susanne encouraged Tom to mend it.
5 Jeff apologized for being late.
6 Gabriela accused Roy of stealing her bike.
7 Erika denied taking the book.
8 Alberto admitted breaking the window.
9 The waiter recommended us to try the pasta.
10 The teacher reminded Nicole to phone her mother.

D Turn the sentences into Reported Questions.
EXAMPLES: 'Who are you?' he asked.
He asked who I was.
'Can you swim?' he asked.
He asked if/whether I could swim.
Notice the change in word order, and the use of *if/whether*.

1 'Can I see you tomorrow, Pat?' asked Lilian.
2 'Who do you think will win, John?' asked David.
3 'How much do I owe you?' Peter asked Mr Black.
4 'Elena, when did you last see Carlos?' asked Jane.
5 'Have you ever been to Delphi?' Vera asked Roger.
6 'Donald, will you be around on Friday?' asked Chantal.
7 'Why didn't he come to school?' asked Michelle.
8 'Does Jonathan like steak?' asked Daniela.
9 'Did they arrive on time?' asked Sally.
10 'Where have you been all morning, Ali?' asked his mother.

E Turn the sentences into Reported Requests or Commands.
EXAMPLES: 'Will you help me with my luggage, John?' asked Sarah.
*Sarah **asked** John **to help** her with her luggage.*
'Don't park here!' said the policeman.
*The policeman **told** us **not to park** there.*

1 'Don't do that!' Liz said to the boy.
2 'Please take a seat, ladies,' said the manager.
3 'Please don't smoke in these seats,' the air hostess said to the passengers.
4 'Would you open the window, Tricia?' said the teacher.
5 'Go up the road and turn first left,' the old man said to the driver.
6 'Hand over the money!' said the bank robber to the clerk.
7 'Leave me alone, all of you!' said Diana.
8 'Can you give me a lift to the airport, Sheila?' said Bill.
9 'Type these letters first,' said Mr Harrap to his secretary.
10 'Patrick, could you possibly lend me £10?' said Mark.

F Complete the sentences, using the correct form of one of these reporting verbs: *accuse, admit, advise, apologize, ask, deny, encourage, recommend, suggest, warn*. Use each verb only once.

1 When he _____ stealing the car, he was arrested.
2 He _____ for being rude yesterday, so we forgave him.
3 We _____ Tony to run in the race, although we didn't think he would win.
4 Janine _____ they should all have coffee at her house.
5 Amanda _____ breaking the plate, but we didn't believe her.
6 The doctor _____ Max to stay in bed for a week.
7 We _____ the policeman how to get to the station.
8 Recently his colleagues _____ him of stealing some money.
9 Yesterday my boss _____ me not to be late again.
10 They _____ me to stay at the Royal Hotel.

I wish and If only

I wish and **If only** are both used when the speaker would like a situation to be different. For a wish about the future, use **would** or **could**:

- *I wish I could go to the party tomorrow.*   (I want to go, but I can't.)
- *If only it would stop raining!*   (Notice the exclamation mark.)

Would is often used when the speaker is complaining about something:

- *I wish she wouldn't use my phone so much.*   • *I wish you would be quiet.*

DO NOT use **I would** or **we would** after **I wish/We wish** or **If only I/If only we**.

For a wish about the present, use a past tense after **I wish** and **If only**:

- *I wish he didn't smoke so much.*   (He smokes a lot.)
- *If only I had a car!*   (But I haven't got one.)

Were instead of **was** is often used after **wish** and **If only**:

- *I wish he were with me now.*

A Complete the sentences, by putting *would* or *could* in the spaces.

1 I wish Andreas _____ help me sometimes.

2 If only I _____ have a holiday!

3 Gavin wished he _____ visit his uncle in Rio de Janeiro.

4 I wish I _____ win the prize.

5 I wish they _____ stop shouting.

6 Judith wishes she _____ go to London for the weekend.

7 If only the baby _____ be quiet for a moment!

8 If only you _____ get the job you want!

B Complete the second sentence so that it has a similar meaning to the first one. Use between two and five words, including the word given. Do not change the word given.

1 I haven't got much money.   MORE
I wish _____ money.

2 She'd like to be far away, on a desert island.   SHE
She wishes _____, on a desert island.

3 Francisco lives a long way away.   SO
I wish Francisco _____ away.

4 I have to practise the piano every day.   ONLY
If _____ to practise the piano every day!

5 I'm not very good at maths.   BETTER
I wish _____ maths.

6 Daniel doesn't live in the centre of town.   LIVE
Daniel wishes he _____ the suburbs.

7 I don't know how to repair the car.   KNEW
If _____ to repair the car!

8 It rains here every day.   RAIN
If only _____ here every day!

For a wish about the past, use the Past Perfect after **wish** and **If only** to express regret:

- *She wishes she had married him.* (But she didn't marry him.)
- *If only I hadn't been so nervous!* (But I was nervous.)

DO NOT use **would have** after **wish** or **If only**.

C Complete the sentences, which refer to the past, using the correct form of the verb in brackets.

1 I wish he _____ so rude yesterday. (not / be)
2 If only Sharon _____ more carefully that day! (drive)
3 They wish they _____ a better job by now. (find)
4 If only I _____ the truth at the time! (know)
5 She wishes she _____ the antique vase. (not / break)
6 I wish I _____ that letter. (not / write)
7 He wishes he _____ the house ten minutes earlier. (leave)
8 We wish we _____ that second-hand car. (not / buy)
9 If only he _____ what we meant! (understand)
10 If only the dog _____ the postman! (not / attack)

D Complete the second sentence so that it has a similar meaning to the first one. Use between two and five words, including the word given. Do not change the word given.

1 Nicholas is sorry he smashed up his car.   WISHES
Nicholas _____ up his car.
2 'Why did I leave my job?' she asked sadly.   LEFT
She wished _____ her job.
3 I'd love to own a horse.   HAD
I _____ a horse.
4 Won't the snow ever stop?   WOULD
If _____ stop!
5 Why didn't we bring an umbrella.   BROUGHT
I _____ an umbrella.
6 Unfortunately I'm not lying on a beach on the Caribbean.   WERE
I _____ on a beach in the Caribbean.
7 I shouldn't have spent so much money.   HADN'T
If _____ so much money!
8 He should stop talking so much.   HE
I _____ so much.
9 I don't think I'll be able to go to the concert.   COULD
If _____ to the concert!
10 I didn't study hard enough last year.   HARDER
If _____ last year!
11 I'd be so happy if Pablo phoned me tonight.   ONLY
If _____ tonight!
12 It's a pity we aren't neighbours.   WE
I _____ neighbours.

The Future

Will and **shall** are used to express

a predictions: • *I think he'll get the job.*
b instant decisions: • *The phone's ringing. I'll answer it.*
c offers of help: • *I'll help you with that, shall I?*
d promises: • *I'll write to you every day.*
e invitations and polite requests: • *Will you come to my party?*

The short forms **I'll** and **we'll** are usually used in spoken English. **Shall** is usually used only with **I** or **we**, and its main use is in offers of help or suggestions:
• *Shall I make you a cup of tea?* • *Shall we book the tickets now?*

The Present Continuous is used for planned future arrangements:
• *He's flying to Zagreb tomorrow.* • *I can't see you tonight. I'm visiting my aunt.*

Going to is used to talk about

a things you intend to do: • *I'm going to save £50 a month for the holiday.*
b predictions based on something in the present:
  • *Look! He's going to win the race.* • *I'm going to be sick.*

The Present Simple is used to talk about timetables, programmes of events and people's schedules:
• *The train leaves at 2.48.* • *What time do we arrive in New York?*

A Complete the dialogue, using the words in brackets.

Pam: What are you doing this weekend?

Sylvie: 1) _____. (visit / cousin / Paris)

Pam: 2) That's nice. _____? (you / fly)

Sylvie: 3) No, I _____. (go / coach)

Pam: 4) _____? (time / it / leave)

Sylvie: 5) At 3.30 today. I _____. (send / you / postcard)

B Complete the sentences with the most natural future form. More than one form may be possible.

1 The President _____ in Atlanta at 5.42. (arrive)
2 You _____ that film. It's too violent. (not / like)
3 She _____ French at university when she leaves school. (study)
4 I _____ some old friends this weekend. (visit)
5 Look at those dark clouds! It _____. (rain)
6 We _____ in the south of Spain as usual this summer. (be)
7 It's rather hot. I _____ the window. (open)
8 I _____ very hard in my new job. I start on Monday. (work)
9 We _____ a car this weekend. (not hire)
10 How old _____ you _____ in December? (be)
11 _____ you _____ me know how much it costs, please? (let)
12 I think I _____ him when I get home. (phone)
13 _____ I _____ you with the washing-up? (help)
14 I know he's in prison, but I _____ him! (see)
15 The photos _____ ready by Wednesday. (be)

Future Continuous and Future Perfect

The Future Continuous is used to talk about a continuous action which will be happening at a particular time in the future:

• *I'll be watching tennis at 2.30 tomorrow.*

The Future Perfect is used to talk about an action which will have happened by a certain point in the future:

• *He will have finished the report by 10 o'clock tonight.*

A Complete the second sentence so that it has a similar meaning to the first one. Use between two and five words, including the word given. Do not change the word given.

1 When I come to school tomorrow, I'm going to wear my glasses.   BE
  Next time you see me, _____ my glasses.

2 Kallitsa is only going to wait for him until 8.15.   WON'T
  At 8.30 Kallitsa _____ for him.

3 He's going to go on writing books all his life.   HE'LL
  In ten years' time _____ books.

4 Ben sets off at 7.30. It takes him an hour to drive to work.   DRIVING
  At 7.45 on Monday morning _____ to work.

5 Fatima does her shopping at about this time every week.   WILL
  This time next week _____ her shopping.

6 We only watch television at the weekend.   BE
  Next Tuesday evening we _____ television.

B Fill the gaps, using the Future Perfect and the correct form of the verb in brackets.

1 By 1999 they _____ married for fifty years. (be)
2 Kate's language course _____ by the end of the year. (finish)
3 The company _____ 10,000 cars before December. (produce)
4 By 5 o'clock this afternoon Linda _____ twenty letters. (type)
5 Matthew _____ 2000 kilometres across the Sahara by next Thursday. (drive)
6 Next time you see me I _____ my exam, I hope. (pass)
7 I'm sorry, but I _____ the report by tonight. (not / finish)
8 _____ you _____ it by tomorrow morning? (finish)

C Complete the dialogue, using the words in brackets and the correct future form.

Brenda: What 1) _____ (you / do) this time next year?

Rosemary: I 2) _____ (study) medicine at university. What about you?

Brenda: Well, I 3) _____ (teach) in Italy. I 4) _____ (finish) my teacher training course by then, you see.

Rosemary: We 5) _____ (not / see) each other for ages. Next time I see you, you 6) _____ (probably / get married) and 7) _____ (have) three children!

Brenda: Well, next time I see *you*, I expect you 8) _____ (discover) a cure for the common cold!

Recycling

A Choose the correct word or phrase to complete each sentence. Write the letter in the space.

1 She suggested _____ for a swim.

   a) go   b) us to go   c) to go   d) we should go

2 They apologized _____ late.

   a) to arriving   b) in arriving   c) for arriving   d) their arriving

3 You're one of Vera's friends, _____ you?

   a) aren't   b) don't   c) won't   d) isn't

4 I told him I _____ the film.

   a) saw already   b) have just seen   c) had seen   d) already seen

5 The guard told the prisoner _____.

   a) not smoking   b) not to smoke   c) no smoking   d) to not smoke

6 I wish I _____ help you, but I can't.

   a) could   b) would   c) can   d) will

7 'I'm _____ an engineer when I grow up,' said the little boy.

   a) being   b) studying   c) going to   d) going to be

8 She wishes she _____ more friends.

   a) would have   b) has   c) had   d) has had

9 _____ we all have a walk in the country?

   a) Let's   b) Shall   c) Will   d) Why not

10 If only I _____ more money!

   a) have saved   b) would have saved   c) would save   d) had saved

11 He's got his visa and he _____ to Chicago tomorrow.

   a) will go   b) going to go   c) is going   d) go

12 I _____ reading this book by next weekend.

   a) will have finished   b) will be finishing   c) have finished
   d) finish

13 We have lived in this town _____ fifteen years.

   a) since   b) for   c) last   d) before

14 She said that if he _____ on time, she would pay him.

   a) arrived   b) would arrive   c) is arriving   d) has arrived

15 This time next week John _____ for me at the airport.

   a) will wait   b) waits   c) will be waiting   d) has waited

16 Julio asked what time the post office _____.

   a) closing   b) to close   c) close   d) closed

17 If you _____ mentioned it, nobody would ever have known.

   a) hadn't   b) wouldn't have   c) didn't   d) shouldn't

18 The convict _____ to have escaped.

   a) is believing   b) is believed   c) believes   d) has been believed

19 As I _____ along the road, I saw a friend of mine.

   a) had cycled   b) was cycling   c) am cycling   d) have cycled

20 Denise suggested that I _____ her.

   a) visiting   b) to visit   c) should visit   d) would visit

B Complete the second sentence so that it has a similar meaning to the first one. Use between two and five words, including the word given. Do not change the word given.

1 'Be careful with your money,' said my father.   TO

My father told _____ with my money.

2 Nobody has ever lived in that house.   NEVER

That house _____ lived in.

3 'If he had asked me, I would have told him the truth,' she said.   HER

She said that if he_____ have told him the truth.

4 People often play tennis on grass courts.   IS

Tennis _____ on grass courts.

5 'Susan, where have you been?' asked her mother.   HAD

Her mother asked _____ been.

6 'Can you come to a barbecue on Saturday, Jim?' asked Mike.   INVITED

Mike _____ barbecue on Saturday.

7 My father intends to resign before the end of the week.   WILL

By the end of the week _____ resigned.

8 I've arranged to fly to Paris this weekend.   AM

This weekend _____ to Paris.

C Read the letter and decide which word or phrase (A, B, C or D) best fits each space.

Dear Thomas,

Thank you for your letters. I've only just 1) _____ time to answer them. I 2) _____ been very busy lately! I 3) _____ the sound of your trip to Portugal. If only I 4) _____ Portuguese! Then I could translate for you!

Next month I 5)_____ my English exams. I'm very nervous about them, because if I 6)_____ pass them, my father won't pay for any more English courses. The other day, he said that 7) _____ I failed, I 8) _____ have to go straight back to Spain. So of course I am 9) _____ very hard at the moment. Now I wish I 10) _____ harder when I first came to England!

Never mind, by the end of June I 11) _____ finished all my exams.

Why 12) _____ you come to London to celebrate with me? Yesterday my teacher told 13) _____ I was looking very pale, so perhaps I 14) _____ studying too much recently!

Best wishes,

Roberto

	A	B	C	D
1	find	found	finding	founded
2	had	was	have	am
3	am liking	liking	would like	like
4	spoke	speak	would speak	spoken
5	will take	going to take	am taking	will be take
6	don't	won't	can	would
7	unless	if	until	while
8	were	will	would	could
9	studying	study	studied	studies
10	did work	would work	worked	had worked
11	will	will have	have	would
12	don't	won't	wouldn't	not
13	for me	to me	me	that
14	have	have been	was	were

UNIT 16

Prepositions

The prepositions **at, in** and **on** are used in expressions of time:
- *at 4.30, at Christmas, at night, at the weekend, on Monday, on 4th June, on my birthday, in the morning/afternoon/evening, in April, in 1972, in (the) spring/summer/autumn/winter*

and in expressions of place:
- *(stay) at home, at 24 Oxford Street, in Birmingham, in Africa, on the beach*

Note that you can **arrive at** or **in** somewhere, but not **to**.

Some important **adjectives and nouns** with their prepositions are:
- *attitude towards, aware of, capable of, confident of, crowded with, difficulty in, envious/jealous of, fed up with, guilty of, intention of, interested in, keen on, key to, point in, possibility of, pride in, proud of, reason for, result of, solution to, surprised at, suspicious of, typical of*

Some common **verbs** with their prepositions are:
- *accuse someone of, apologize for, blame someone for, concentrate on, congratulate someone on, depend on, forgive someone for, insist on, object to, prevent someone/something from, succeed in*

The **-ing** form is normally used after an adjective, noun or verb plus preposition:
- *We forgave him for lying to us.*

Note that there is **no preposition** after these verbs:
- *ring, phone, discuss, divorce, marry, lack, tell*

A Complete the phrases with the correct preposition: *at, in* or *on*.

1 _____ Midsummer's Day
2 _____ 1922
3 _____ Frankfurt Airport
4 _____ spring
5 arrive _____ Asia
6 _____ January
7 _____ the afternoon
8 _____ midnight
9 _____ 4th May 1999
10 _____ Tuesday
11 _____ night
12 _____ Friday morning
13 arrive _____ Victoria Station
14 _____ Chinese New Year
15 stay _____ home
16 _____ 221b Baker Street

B Match the two halves of the sentences correctly.

1 She accused me
2 The bus was crowded
3 We have absolutely no intention
4 There is really no point
5 I suppose you insisted
6 She strongly objects
7 I am confident
8 He's keen
9 She has no valid reason
10 You'd better concentrate

A of success.
B on seeing the manager?
C of stealing her handbag.
D of leaving yet.
E for resigning.
F on collecting musical instruments
G with late-night shoppers.
H on your homework.
I to people smoking in her office.
J in making a fuss.

C Some of the lines in this letter are correct, and others have a word which should not be there. Tick any lines which are correct. Write down any words which should not be there.

Everybody knew that Rory hardly ever arrived to anywhere on time.	1
However, he was determined to be punctual for his boss's wedding.	2
Mr Taylor had divorced from his first wife, and was planning to	3
marry with a colleague. He was proud of his rapport with his staff,	4
and insisted on that as many as possible should attend. Rory's first	5
problem was that he was going to another wedding earlier in the	6
day, so he rang to Mr Taylor's secretary to let her know he couldn't	7
attend the ceremony, but would get there in the time for the	8
reception at the Savoy Hotel. 'Typical for of you!' she said. 'You're	9
always late!' 'I'll be there!' he told to her rather crossly.	10
Unfortunately, at the first wedding he spent so long discussing	11
about the past with old friends that he had to take a taxi to the	12
Savoy, and when he was arrived, the reception was almost over. It	13
seemed the newlyweds had already left on their honeymoon, so he	14
couldn't even apologize them for arriving late.	15

The same **preposition** is often used after adjectives or verbs with a similar or opposite meaning. Look at the following examples:

care) **about** the child worry) be anxious)	good) **at** swimming bad)	apply) **for** information send) ask)
ready) **for** school prepared)	approve) **of** his friends disapprove)	frightened) **of** the dog afraid) scared)
married) **to** that girl engaged) related)	angry) **with** him annoyed) cross) irritated) furious)	agree) **with** them disagree)

D Complete the passage, using the correct prepositions.

At 16, Paul decided he was ready 1) _____ full-time work, and left school. At first his parents did not agree 2) _____ him, and wanted him to stay on to finish his studies. In fact, they were very angry 3) _____ him. 'We're worried 4) _____ your future!' his father told him. 'How can you ever get a good job if you leave school and sit in cafés, drinking coffee with your friends?' His parents strongly disapproved 5) _____ Paul's friends. But Paul was determined to prove them wrong, and so he applied 6) _____ dozens of jobs. In the end he was offered a job in an accountant's office, because he was good 7) _____ maths. In his spare time he studied accountancy. His parents soon realized that he wasn't wasting time with his friends, and they got used 8) _____ his new life-style. When, a few years later, he became engaged 9) _____ the accountant's daughter, they were delighted, and when he passed his accountancy exams and became a partner in the firm, they were very proud 10) _____ him.

UNIT 17

Comparatives and Superlatives

The comparative of most short adjectives and adverbs is formed by adding **(e)r**:
- *a larger car* • *a quieter house* • *She works harder.*

If the adjective ends with one vowel and one consonant, double the consonant to form the comparative: • *a thinner cat* • *a bigger dog* • *a fatter woman*

With longer adjectives and all adverbs ending in **– ly**, use **more** to form the comparative:
- *a more satisfied customer* • *She dances more gracefully than her sister.*

Some two-syllable adjectives add **– er**, and some add **more** to form the comparative:
- *modern / more modern* • *clever / cleverer*

Than is used to compare two things:
- *Arabic is more difficult to learn than Spanish.*

A bit, a little, even, much, a lot, and **far** can all be used before a comparative:

- *She's a lot happier than she was last year.*

Note these irregular comparatives:
- *good/well better* • *far further/farther* • *bad/badly worse*

and these comparisons: • *Zora is taller than Susan.* • *Susan isn't as tall as Zora.*

A Complete the sentences, using the correct form of one of these adjectives or adverbs: *peaceful, easy, big, comfortable, beautiful, long, important, slowly, frightened.*

1 English is _____ to learn _____ Danish.
2 My feet are size 42: they're _____ yours.
3 Simon drives _____ his friend Paul.
4 Our discussion was far _____ you think.
5 My armchair is a bit _____ yours.
6 Living in the country is _____ living in town.
7 My cousin is much _____ that film star.
8 Adel's letter is _____ Ahmed's.

B Complete the second sentence so that it has a similar meaning to the first one. Use between two and five words, including the word given. Do not change the word given.

1 Liz drinks more milk than Gregory.   MUCH
   Gregory doesn't_____ Liz.
2 Rachel doesn't cook as well as Helen.   THAN
   Helen cooks_____ Rachel.
3 My father is taller than yours.   TALL
   Your father_____ mine.
4 We don't live as far from Tokyo as he does.   LIVES
   He _____ than we do.
5 Mr Brown has fewer holidays than he used to.   MANY
   Mr Brown _____ holidays as he used to.
6 Pedro's typing isn't as bad as Manuel's.   TYPING
   Manuel's _____ Pedro's.

> The **superlative** of most short adjectives and adverbs is formed with **the + – est**.
> **The most** is used with longer words:
>
> • *the tallest person*   • *the most expensive hotel*   • *Jim speaks the most fluently.*
>
> The rules are the same as for comparatives.
>
> Note these irregular superlatives:
>
> • *best*   • *worst*   • *furthest*
>
> A superlative is often followed by **in**:   • *the highest mountain in the world*
> Exception: • *the happiest / worst day of my life*   • *the youngest of her brothers*
>
> A superlative is often followed by a perfect tense:
>
> • *'The Silence of the Lambs' is the most frightening film I've ever seen.*
> • *It was the worst meal I had ever eaten.*
>
> Note these sentences, which all mean the same:
>
> • *It's the worst experience I've ever had.*
> • *I've never had such a bad experience (before).*
> • *I've never had an experience as bad as that (before).*

C Complete the sentences with the correct superlative.

1 The Sahara is _____ desert in the world. (large)
2 She was _____ girl I had ever seen. (beautiful)
3 It's _____ camera in the shop. (expensive)
4 That's _____ question to answer. (easy)
5 It was _____ day of my life. (bad)
6 This textbook is _____ to understand. (difficult)
7 He's _____ film star in my country. (popular)
8 The Queen of England is one of _____ women in the world. (rich)

D Complete the second sentence so that it has a similar meaning to the first one. Use between two and five words, including the word given. Do not change the word given.

1 He's the best player our team has ever had.   NEVER
Our team _____ good player.
2 Nobody in my family drives as badly as he does.   THE
He's_____ my family.
3 That's the most hurtful thing anybody has ever said to me.   SUCH
Nobody has_____ thing to me.
4 I've never lived in such a big town before.   FIRST
It's the_____ lived in such a big town.
5 I haven't tasted such good coffee for ages.   BEST
This is _____ tasted for ages.
6 None of the other books is as interesting as this one.   MOST
This book _____one.
7 Rachel is the most generous person I know.   MORE
I don't know _____ Rachel.
8 That's the cheapest dish on the menu.   AS
None of the other dishes _____ one.

Have something done

> **Have something done** is used when someone arranges for something to be done by someone else:
> - *I'm going to have my house painted.* (Someone is going to do it for me.)
>
> The word order is important:
> **have** (correct tense) + **object** + **past participle** (of relevant verb).

A Match each object in the first column with an action in the second column. Write the correct letter next to the number on the right.

I'm going to have

1	my hair	A	serviced	1	____
2	my house	B	mended / repaired	2	____
3	my shoes	C	typed	3	____
4	my suit	D	redecorated	4	____
5	the letters	E	cut	5	____
6	my car	F	dry-cleaned	6	____

B Complete the sentences, practising the causative use of *have*. Use the correct form of the verb in brackets.

1 Mary didn't make the dress herself. She _____. (make)

2 Your hair looks much shorter. Have you _____? (cut)

3 I can't repair the camera myself so I'm _____. (repair)

4 The car isn't running well. We ought to _____ before we go on holiday. (service)

5 Those coats are very dirty. You'd better _____. (clean)

6 You really need central heating. You could easily _____. (install)

7 I've bought a new carpet for the living-room and this afternoon I'm _____. (fit)

8 Those are my favourite boots. I hope I'll be able to _____. (mend)

9 He thought he had broken his arm, so he went to hospital to _____. (X-ray)

10 I'm worried about the brakes on my car, so I think I'll _____. (check)

C Some of these sentences are not correct. Tick (✓) the right ones, and correct the wrong ones.

1 Sue had washed her hair by the hairdresser.

2 Hazel had always wanted to have a dress designed especially for her.

3 Have you had a meal cooked for you?

4 Robert is going to have serviced his car by the local mechanic.

5 They're having cut down the trees by the workmen.

6 She had the curtains cleaned.

7 I couldn't understand the letter, so I had translated it.

8 He had taken his photo by a famous photographer.

9 They usually have a newspaper delivered in the morning.

10 I haven't had my film developed yet.

Definite and Indefinite Articles

The definite article **the** is used with a noun when it is clear which noun we mean:
• *I live in the house next to the shop.*

The indefinite article **a/an** is used when a noun is referred to for the first time, or when it is not clear which noun we mean: • *There was a girl in the street.*

The is also used with musical instruments, some adjectives with plural meanings, some nationality adjectives, most mountain ranges, oceans, seas, rivers, plural names of countries, island groups and regions, and to talk about a whole species:

• *play the piano*   • *the old*   • *the French*   • *the Far East*   • *the panda*

No article is used when generalizing, or with most countries, towns, streets, etc. and lakes: • *I like rice*   • *Trafalgar Square*   • *Lake Victoria*

Unless a particular one is meant, no article is used before *college, university, school, prison, hospital* or *church*. Notice also:
• *go to bed, stay in bed, go to work, start work, go home, stay at home*

A Complete the passage with the correct article, *the, a* or *an.*

I saw 1) ____ marvellous film yesterday. It's about 2) ____ poor fisherman who's in love with 3) ____ beautiful girl. She laughs at him when he asks her to marry him but 4) ____ young man doesn't give up hope. One night there's 5) ____ terrible storm. All 6) ____ fishing-boats have come home safely, except one. 7) ____ missing boat belongs to 8) ____ girl's brother. She begs 9) ____ poor fisherman to brave 10) ____ huge waves to try and save her brother, and when he returns with 11) ____ boy, safe and sound, 12) ____ girl is so grateful that she agrees to marry him. There is 13) ____ big wedding party, and all 14) ____ villagers join in 15) ____ celebrations. What 16) ____ happy ending!

B Complete the sentences with *the* or no article (–).

1   Salem doesn't like ____ talkative people.
2   It's true that ____ rich lead a different life from ____ poor.
3   Helmut lives in ____ Canada near ____ Lake Ontario.
4   The explorer crossed ____ Pacific Ocean in a canoe.
5   She has been playing ____ flute for ten years.
6   For breakfast we usually have ____ coffee and toast.
7   What time do you start ____ work in the morning?
8   Eileen hopes to go to ____ university next year.
9   We went on a cruise down ____ Nile and saw ____ Pyramids.
10   Sarah thinks ____ life is more difficult in a foreign country.
11   The judge sentenced the pickpocket to six months in ____ prison.
12   I've noticed that ____ Spanish eat a lot of vegetables.
13   A volcano has erupted in ____ Philippines recently.
14   ____ examinations always make him nervous.

Recycling

A Choose the correct word or phrase to complete each sentence. Write the letter in the space.

1 Adel usually goes to the cinema _____ the evening.
   a) in   b) at   c) on   d) of

2 The headmaster disapproved _____ his behaviour.
   a) with   b) by   c) on   d) of

3 There's no point _____ his work for him.
   a) to do   b) to doing   c) in doing   d) with doing

4 Did Karen marry _____ your cousin in the end?
   a) to   b) with   c) -   d) him

5 He takes great pride _____ all his achievements
   a) of   b) in   c) with   d) for

6 Madrid is _____ bigger than Granada.
   a) much   b) bit   c) lot   d) many

7 That was the happiest day _____ my life.
   a) all   b) of   c) in   d) for

8 She warned the child _____ the busy road.
   a) not crossing   b) to cross   c) to not cross   d) not to cross

9 Did you _____ those photos last year?
   a) took   b) taken   c) take   d) taking

10 My sister is very good _____ history.
   a) in   b) at   c) for   d) to

11 We were exhausted by the time we arrived _____ Beirut.
   a) in   b) to   c) at   d) -

12 Your car is in _____ condition than mine.
   a) worse   b) worst   c) bad   d) badly

13 Very few passenger ships cross _____ Atlantic these days.
   a) –   b) an   c) Ocean   d) the

14 If the weather _____ bad, we'll go to the cinema.
   a) will be   b) were   c) is   d) would be

15 I didn't buy the book because I _____ it.
   a) already read   b) will read   c) read   d) had already read

16 When I arrived late, my boss was very angry _____ me.
   a) with   b) for   c) to   d) of

17 If you are tired, you should _____ bed.
   a) go   b) go to   c) go to the   d) go in the

18 The new school _____ last year.
   a) has opened   b) is opened   c) was opened   d) was opening

19 I think you need to have _____.
   a) your television repaired   b) repaired your television
   c) television repaired   d) repair your television

20 Maria walks _____ than her sister.
   a) slowly   b) more slow   c) slower   d) more slowly

B Complete the second sentence so that it has a similar meaning to the first one. Use between two and five words, including the word given. Do not change the word given.

1 Her parents don't like her coming home late.   APPROVE

Her parents _____ home late.

2 People say that Prague is a wonderful city.   SUPPOSED

Prague _____ a wonderful city.

3 'I'm terribly sorry I'm late,' said Flora.   APOLOGIZED

Flora _____ late.

4 Your brother is more intelligent than mine.   AS

My brother_____ yours.

5 I've never seen such a beautiful sunset before.   I

That's the _____ ever seen.

6 Dimitri paid someone to repair his CD player.   HAD

Dimitri _____ repaired.

7 When I lent him the money, I had no idea he was rich.   KNOWN

If I _____ , I wouldn't have lent him the money.

8 Rolf was sad because he had no brothers or sisters.   WISHED

Rolf _____ brothers or sisters.

C Some of the lines in this letter are correct, and others have a word which should not be there. Tick any lines which are correct. Write down any words which should not be there.

Dear Roberto,

Thanks for your letter. Good luck in your exams. When you will	1
pass them, you'll be able to stay in to England. Just remember that!	2
I've just been had my car repaired by a mechanic. It was very	3
expensive! £800! I really wish I had more enough money to buy a	4
new one. I think I'd like buy a sports car this time!	5
One another thing I'd like to do is travel more. My friend John is	6
planning to go on summer holiday soon. He wants to cycle over the	7
Pyrenees, through the Spain and then go across the Mediterranean	8
by a boat. He expects to arrive in the Middle East in two months'	9
time. I only wish I could go with him.	10
I hope to come to London for a weekend in at June. Maybe you	11
can get a tickets for a musical like Les Misérables?	12

Best wishes,

Thomas

Difficult Verbs

Make someone do something means to oblige or force them:

• *My parents made me study hard when I was young.* (active)
• *I was made to study hard when I was young.* (passive)

Let and **allow** mean to give permission for something to happen:

• *He let me drive his car.* • *He allowed me to drive his car.* (active)
• *I was allowed to drive his car.* (passive)

Notice that there is no **to** before the infinitive in the active construction with **make** or **let**. There is no passive construction for **let**.

Generally speaking, **do** is used with nouns expressing work, a duty or an obligation:

• *do your homework* • *do the washing-up*

When **make** is used with nouns, it often means to produce or create something new, which did not exist before:

• *make a cake* • *make a plan* • *make a mistake*

A Complete the second sentence so that it has a similar meaning to the first one. Use between two and five words, including the word given. Do not change the word given.

1 He will be allowed to leave prison soon. **LET**
They _____ prison soon.

2 The authorities forced my brother to join the army. **MADE**
My brother _____ the army.

3 Her mother lets her get up late on holiday. **ALLOWED**
She _____ late on holiday.

4 We had to do the housework because they told us to. **WERE**
We _____ the housework.

5 I'll have the right to vote when I'm eighteen. **ME**
They'll _____ when I'm eighteen.

6 Duncan wasn't allowed to join the squash club. **LET**
They _____ the squash club.

7 The student will be obliged to apologize. **MAKE**
They'll _____ apologize.

8 My parents don't allow me to smoke at home. **AM**
I _____ at home.

B Complete the sentences with the correct form of *do* or *make*.

1 Despite his lack of experience, he _____ his job very well.

2 Don't worry, that's a mistake that everybody _____.

3 I think his mother has already _____ the shopping.

4 Charles will have to _____ his military service next year.

5 Have you _____ that maths exercise yet?

6 Stuart _____ a fortune by buying up small companies.

7 They usually _____ the housework on Saturday morning.

8 The director will be asked to _____ a speech at the ceremony.

Used to do expresses a habit in the past which is finished now. In this expression, used to is a verb in the Past Simple:

- *We used to wear uniform at school.* • *I didn't use to like curry.*

Be/get used to doing means to be/get accustomed to doing something, or to acquire a habit over a long time. In these expressions, used is like an adjective:

- *Antonetta has got used to eating dinner late in Spain.*
  (This was rather strange for her when she first arrived.)

Be/get used to can also be followed by a noun:

- *It took her a long time to get used to the food.*

Lie (lying), lied, lied means not to tell the truth: • *He's always lying to people.*
Lie (lying), lay, lain means to be horizontal: • *She lay there in the sun for hours.*
Lay (laying), laid, laid means to put something down: • *He laid the child gently on the ground.*
Note: • *lay the table, lay an egg*

Rise (rising), rose, risen takes no object: • *Prices rose last year.*
Raise (raising), raised, raised takes an object: • *He raised his hand.*

C Match the two halves of the sentences correctly.

1 The mayor laid
2 I'm sure he's never lied
3 The congregation all rose
4 The blackbird laid

5 Inflation has been rising
6 The company may raise
7 Take an aspirin and lie
8 The stones have lain

A as the bride entered the church.
B in the grass for centuries.
C workers' salaries this year.
D the foundation stone for the new school.
E down for a few minutes.
F steadily for several years.
G to his parents.
H three eggs in the nest.

D Complete the sentences, using *used to* or *be/get used to* and the correct form of the verb in brackets if there is one.

1 When Ted was on holiday, he _____ in the sea every morning. (swim)
2 Ahmed has _____ in English shops. (queue)
3 I've lived in Italy for years, so I'm _____ a lot of pasta. (eat)
4 Barbara goes everywhere by car now, but she _____ by bike. (travel)
5 My cousin only listens to classical music these days, but she _____ to pop music all the time. (listen)
6 Don't worry. You'll soon _____ the climate.
7 Amir doesn't watch television much now, but he _____ a lot when he was younger. (watch)
8 My father is _____ at 7.30. He's been doing it for thirty years. (get up)
9 Where did you _____ before you moved to Barcelona? (live)
10 I didn't _____ jazz, but now I do. (like)

Relative Pronouns

Who is used to refer to a person: • *The girl who phoned is my sister.*

Which and **that** are used to refer to a thing:

• *The house which you saw belongs to the President.*

What means 'the thing that': • *I told him what happened.*

Whose is used instead of **his/her/their**: • *That's the man whose car was stolen.*

Whom can be used formally instead of **who** when it is the object of the verb, but **who** is more common in spoken English:

• *People whom the company employs are expected to sign a contract.*

Where is used to refer to a particular place: • *That's the house where I was born.*

If **who**, **which** or **that** is the subject of the relative clause, the pronoun is important and must be kept, but if it is the object, the pronoun may be left out:

• *He's the boy who invited me to play tennis.*
• *Have you found the book (which / that) you lost?*

A Complete the sentences with the correct relative pronoun.

1 That's the man _____ helped me yesterday.
2 Please don't tell him _____ I said.
3 The house _____ overlooks the sea is Nayla's.
4 That's the village _____ my mother was born.
5 Did you see the people _____ money we found?
6 Anyone _____ arrives late will be punished
7 Did he explain _____ went wrong?
8 He's the painter _____ last exhibition was such a failure.
9 I read the magazine _____ was lying on the table.
10 It was my teacher _____ told me to do the exercise.

B Join each pair of sentences to make one sentence. Use a relative pronoun only if you need to.
EXAMPLE: I've lost the earrings. I bought them on holiday. *I've lost the earrings I bought on holiday.*

1 She put on the clothes. She had bought them the day before.
2 I wanted to see the man. He owned the restaurant.
3 There are lots of interesting places. I'd like to visit them.
4 That's the boy. My brother plays basketball with him.
5 I'm looking forward to the programme. It's on after the news.
6 Do you remember the hotel in Edinburgh? Your parents stayed there last year.
7 Those are the shoes. I cleaned them for you.
8 He's written down the word. He looked it up yesterday.
9 That's the old lady. Her brother won the Nobel Prize.
10 I've lost the list. I had it in my hand a moment ago.

Defining relative clauses give us the necessary information to know which person or thing is referred to:

- *The man who bought my car can't drive.*

In defining relative clauses, **that** is often used instead of **which** after superlatives, **all**, **every(thing)**, **nothing**, **any(thing)**, **some(thing)**, **none**, **little**, **few**, **much** and **only**:

- *That's the worst play that has ever been performed here.*
- *The only thing that matters is to tell the truth.*

If it is the object, the relative pronoun is often left out:

- *He did everything he could to help.*

Non-defining relative clauses give extra information which is not really necessary:

- *Anita's aunt, who is forty-five, lives in Alexandria.*

That cannot be used, and the relative pronoun cannot be left out. A comma must be used before this kind of relative clause, and also after it if it is in the middle of a sentence:

- *I gave the girl an apple, which she ate immediately.*

C Join each pair of sentences, using a relative pronoun. Use commas if necessary.

1 He gave me the information. I wrote it down at once.
2 Andrea went to see the dentist. He took out two of her teeth.
3 Fritz lives in the house round the corner. It has a red front door.
4 Show me the shoes. You bought them yesterday.
5 Have you seen the film? It's on at the Odeon.
6 My boyfriend refused to go to the concert with me. He hates country music.
7 We climbed to the top of the mountain. We had a picnic there.
8 Edward has just moved to France. His mother died last year.
9 We didn't want to swim in the sea. It looked very dirty.
10 Lydia is reading that fascinating book on Spanish history. You lent it to her last week.

D Complete the second sentence so that it has a similar meaning to the first one. Use between two and five words, including the word given. Do not change the word given.

1 You can do nothing to make me change my mind.   IS
  There _____ to make me change my mind.
2 A better film about love has never been made.   BEST
  It's the _____ has ever been made.
3 None of the specially prepared food was left over.   ATE
  The guests _____ had been especially prepared.
4 I've never seen a bigger dog than that one.   EVER
  That's the _____ seen.
5 The company has produced a lot of sports cars, and has sold them all.   BY
  All the sports cars _____ been sold.
6 Whatever has been ordered will be delivered.   EVERYTHING
  We will deliver _____ ordered.

Some, Any, Much, Many, Little, Few, A lot

Some and words beginning with **some–** are usually used in positive sentences:

- *I'd love some cake.* • *Somebody must have seen the thief.*

Any– words are usually used in negative sentences, in questions, and after **if**:

- *We haven't got any bread.* • *If anyone knocks, just open the door.*

Any– words can also mean that it is not important who, which etc:

- *'Where shall we go?' 'Anywhere, I don't mind.'*
- *Anyone who has registered can attend lessons.*

We often use **some** in questions if we expect the answer **yes**, especially when offering or asking for things. Compare: *Have you got any fruit?* and *Would you like some fruit?*

Much and **little** are used with uncountable nouns, while **many** and **few** are used with plural countable nouns:

- *much/little money* • *many/few friends*

A lot of can be used with either countable or uncountable nouns:

- *a lot of money* • *a lot of friends*

A lot of is usually used in positive sentences, especially in spoken English, instead of **much** and **many**, which are mainly used in negative sentences and questions:

- *A lot of people came to the party. Unfortunately, there wasn't much food.*

A little and **a few** mean a small amount or number, but **little** and **few** mean not enough. **Very** is used to stress **little** and **few**:

- *I've got a little money left, so I can buy some postcards.*
- *He won't get the job because he has very few qualifications.*

A Complete the sentences with *some, any, somebody, something, somewhere, anybody, anything* or *anywhere*.

1 There's _____ expensive furniture in his house.

2 Haven't you got _____ brothers or sisters at all?

3 Let's stay at home this evening. I don't want to go _____.

4 _____ told me the factory would close down soon.

5 If there are _____ problems, just ask me for help.

6 You can catch _____ train from Platform 3. They all go to London.

7 Could I have _____ tomatoes, please?

8 I've got _____ important to tell you.

9 You can invite _____ you like. I don't mind.

10 I haven't done _____ work yet.

11 Didn't you discuss _____ interesting at the meeting?

12 I'm not sure where she lives. It's _____ in Scotland, I think.

13 _____ must have seen what happened.

14 _____ who has a complaint should see the manager.

B Underline the uncountable nouns in the list.

furniture   knowledge   banana   student   luggage
books   information   milk   people   butter
suitcase   meat   cheese   water   cattle
news   money   vegetable   litres   advice

C Complete the sentences with *much, many, (a) few, (a) little* or *a lot of.*

1 He's got five suitcases! What _____ luggage!
2 Our house is almost empty because we haven't got _____ furniture.
3 The lawyer gave me _____ advice, but not enough to solve my problem.
4 How _____ brothers has Pepe got?
5 There were only _____ students in my class last week, because most of them were ill.
6 How _____ time is there left before the end of the match?
7 Life is difficult for Andy because he earns very _____ money.
8 There were _____ people in the theatre, which was more crowded than usual.
9 _____ people enjoy going to the dentist.
10 Martha has only had a passport for two years, so she hasn't visited _____ countries.

D Underline the correct alternative in each sentence.

1 There isn't *any / some* lemonade left in the bottle.
2 David has *a lot of / much* friends at school.
3 There's only *a few / a little* news in my letter.
4 There aren't *many / much* vegetables in the garden.
5 Only *a little / a few* people know the answer to that question.
6 Ramon hasn't got *much / many* homework tonight.
7 Would you like *some / much* milk in your tea?
8 The tourist office gave us *a lot of / many* useful information about coach tours.
9 I asked my teacher for *a little / a few* advice.
10 Sit down. I've got *a few / few* things to say to you.
11 Wasn't there *few / any* petrol in the car?
12 There was *very little / not a little* for the children to do.

E Match the two correct halves of the sentences. Write the correct letter next to the number on the right.

1 How much   A potatoes did you buy?   1 ____
2 There isn't much   B information did you get?   2 ____
3 There are very few   C time left.   3 ____
4 We didn't buy any   D waiters in the restaurant.   4 ____
5 How many   E fruit last week.   5 ____

Now do the same for the rest of the exercise.

6 I've prepared some   F work so far.   6 ____
7 He has found little   G sandwiches, has he?   7 ____
8 She's invited a lot of   H food with you?   8 ____
9 Have you got any   I delicious soup for you.   9 ____
10 John hasn't eaten many   J friends to dinner.   10 ____

Gerund and Infinitive

The verbs **want** and **would like** (meaning *want*) always take the infinitive:

- *She wanted to get a job.*   • *He would like to go to Africa.*

The following verbs usually take the infinitive: **promise, encourage, warn, remind, decide, agree, refuse, offer, help, manage, tend**:

- *They helped me to decorate the living-room.*

The following verbs usually take the gerund: **spend/waste (time), finish, dread, detest, hate, avoid, dislike, risk, deny, postpone, like, love, enjoy, imagine, understand, mind, consider, miss**:

- *She enjoys sailing in her spare time.*   • *Would you mind coming with me?*

Adjectives with prepositions always take the gerund:

- *fond of singing*   • *keen on learning Spanish*   • *fed up with studying*

Most **phrasal verbs** and **verbs with particles** also take the gerund:

- *He put off making the appointment.*   • *She apologized for being late.*

Other common expressions which normally take the gerund are: **can't risk, can't stand, can't bear, it's no use, it's (not) worth**.

A Complete the sentences with the infinitive or the gerund of the verb in brackets.

1 Patrick is putting on weight. He'll have to give up _____ snacks. (eat)

2 I can't stand people _____ me questions all the time. (ask)

3 Her brother is very keen on _____. (swim)

4 His boss wants him _____ harder. (work)

5 Sandra promised _____ Peter with his packing. (help)

6 It's a very long flight to New Zealand. It's not worth _____ for less than a fortnight. (go)

7 I'm afraid I'm very bad at _____ languages. (learn)

8 The driver only just avoided _____ the dog. (hit)

9 Demetrio is fed up with _____ a student. (be)

10 She forgave her sister for _____ her. (deceive)

11 Although we tried to stop him, he kept on _____. (talk)

12 Would you like _____ tennis with me? (play)

13 It was a difficult exam, but Jennifer managed _____ it. (pass)

14 The snow prevented the train from _____ on time. (arrive)

15 Since coming here, I've got used to _____ to bed early. (go)

16 The old lady accused the boy of _____ her handbag. (steal)

17 Jane is looking forward to _____ three weeks in California. (spend)

18 I don't mind _____ up early, if I have to. (get)

19 It's no use _____ him. He isn't interested. (tell)

20 Last summer we decided _____ overland through India. (travel)

> **The gerund**, because it is like a noun, can also be used as the subject of a sentence:
>
> • *Looking after children needs patience.*   • *Getting up early can be difficult.*
>
> It is also used after **come** and **go**:
>
> • *Let's go shopping tomorrow.*   • *Would you like to come swimming?*
>
> The verbs **remember**, **forget**, **need**, **try**, **stop**, **go on** take either the gerund or the infinitive, depending on the meaning required:
>
> • *I remember seeing him last week.*   • *Remember to give him the present when you see him.*
> • *We need to get visas to enter Canada.*   • *His car needs repairing.*
> • *I'll never forget seeing the forest fire.*   • *Don't forget to lock the door.*
> • *He tried to start the car, but it had run out of petrol.*   • *Try turning the key first and then pushing the door.*
> • *Stop talking at once!*   • *He stopped to look at the shop window.*
> • *She went on talking until the bell rang.*   • *He went on to explain why he had come.*

B Complete the sentences with the infinitive or the gerund of the verb in brackets.

1 Don't forget _____ him for coffee when you see him. (invite)
2 First he repaired the radio, then he went on _____ the television. (repair)
3 Their house really needs _____. (paint)
4 Her aunt remembers _____ the first car in her village. (see)
5 Ken always likes _____ on holiday to hot countries. (go)
6 They stopped the car _____ a chat with their friends. (have)
7 Go on _____. It's very interesting. (explain)
8 Why don't you try _____ your breath, or _____ a glass of water? (hold, drink)
9 Will he remember _____ the bill? I told him he should do it today. (pay)
10 _____ old bottles is a strange hobby. (collect)
11 He stopped _____ because he was sleepy. (drive)
12 He'll soon forget _____ involved in the accident. (be)
13 Liz needs _____ a job. She's short of money. (get)
14 They tried _____ their way, but they were lost. (find)
15 Shall we go _____ tomorrow morning? (run)

C Some of the sentences are not correct. Tick (✔) the right ones, and correct the wrong ones.

1 Pedro enjoys to have a coffee after dinner.
2 Edward tends to do things at the last possible moment.
3 Sylvie spent three weeks to revise for her exams.
4 These shoes need to mend, don't you think?
5 We encouraged him applying for the job.
6 Judy didn't finish writing the letter until midnight.
7 He risked to offend her by telling her what he thought.
8 I think you need to buy a warm coat.
9 Roger has always hated living in a town.
10 Would you consider to work for a different company?

Recycling

A Choose the correct word or phrase to complete each sentence. Write the letter in the space.

1 It's the best book _____ I've ever read.

   a) which   b) who   c) that   d) what

2 I used to _____ to London more often than I do now.

   a) driving   b) driven   c) drove   d) drive

3 The boy was made _____ his homework.

   a) to do   b) do   c) doing   d) to doing

4 Stormy weather prevented the ferry _____ the crossing.

   a) from making   b) to make   c) with making   d) by making

5 Will you be able to come to our party _____ Monday 24th July?

   a) in   b) on   c) at   d) the

6 Fred sometimes helps his mother to _____ the housework.

   a) make   b) making   c) do   d) doing

7 Sophie _____ eat a lot of sweets when she was young.

   a) was used to   b) usually   c) did use   d) used to

8 I hope they'll concentrate _____ their computer skills.

   a) for improving   b) on improving   c) to improve   d) to improving

9 I told the policeman _____ had happened.

   a) which   b) who   c) what   d) that

10 That's the businessman _____ company is so successful.

   a) whose   b) who's   c) who   d) which

11 The boy denied _____ the window.

   a) broken   b) breaking   c) to break   d) break

12 Is that the town _____ you were born?

   a) which   b) that   c) whose   d) where

13 She can't bear people _____ at her.

   a) shouting   b) to shout   c) shout   d) shouted

14 You can go _____ you like. This isn't private land.

   a) nowhere   b) somewhere   c) anywhere   d) there

15 He arrived at the hotel with only _____ luggage.

   a) a little   b) a few   c) any   d) a lot of

16 Could I have _____ sugar in my tea, please?

   a) any   b) some   c) little   d) few

17 How _____ information did you ask for?

   a) many   b) lot   c) some   d) much

18 Would you like _____ my dictionary?

   a) borrowing   b) borrow   c) to borrow   d) borrowed

19 Irene's very keen _____ Spanish.

   a) on learning   b) to learning   c) on learn   d) at learning

20 She remembers _____ after you when you were a baby.

   a) look   b) to look   c) looking   d) have looked

B Complete the second sentence so that it has a similar meaning to the first one. Use between two and five words, including the word given. Do not change the word given.

1 It took me four hours to do my homework.   SPENT

I _____ my homework.

2 Ursula often goes away for the weekend.   TENDS

Ursula _____ for the weekend.

3 I think you should join a health club.   WERE

If _____ join a health club.

4 There weren't many people watching the match.   FEW

Only _____ watching the match.

5 'I'll give the money back tomorrow,' said Philip.   PROMISED

Philip _____ back the next day.

6 Elisa's parents never let her stay out late.   ALLOWED

Elisa is _____ out late.

7 It'll be lovely to see all our friends this evening.   FORWARD

We're _____ all our friends this evening.

8 He should take those shoes to be mended soon.   HAVE

He should _____ soon.

C Read the letter and decide which word or phrase (A, B, C or D) best fits each space.

Dear Thomas,

Thank you for your letter. I think I can remember 1) _____ John. His bike must be a lot better 2) _____ mine, 3) _____ certainly wouldn't take me all the way to 4) _____ Middle East!

I have 5) _____ great news for you. Today I received my exam results, and I 6) _____ passed them all! So this evening I 7) _____ my father, who 8) _____ I could stay in England for another six months. He also told 9) _____ to invite you to Spain. He's keen on me 10) _____ English friends, you see, and 11) _____ to meet you. So when you 12) _____ to London next weekend, we can discuss the trip.

I've just bought the tickets 13) _____ asked me to get, but they were 14) _____ expensive than I expected. Never mind, I'm sure we'll enjoy the show.

See you soon.

Best wishes,

Roberto

	A	B	C	D
1	meeting	meet	to meet	have met
2	then	than	as	like
3	who	that	which	it
4	a	the	-	that
5	some	a	extremely	several
6	had	has	have	was
7	ring	rung	rang	ringing
8	told	said	allowed	informed
9	me	that	please	them
10	to have	have	has	having
11	wanting	is wanting	wants	want
12	come	will come	arrive	came
13	that	which	they	you
14	less	more	very	so

UNIT 26

Conjunctions

The linking words or conjunctions **although, however, but, despite, in spite of, even though** and **though** are used with different structures:
- *Although it was raining, he went for a walk.*
- *It was raining. However, he went for a walk.*
- *It was raining, but he went for a walk.*
- *Despite the rain/In spite of the rain he went for a walk.*
- *In spite of/Despite the fact that it was raining, he went for a walk.*
- *Even though it was raining, he went for a walk.* (a stronger form of **although)**
- *It was raining. He went for a walk, though.* (more common in spoken English)

Note that **despite** and **in spite of** can only be followed by a noun or gerund. The gerund can only be used if the subject of both parts of the sentence is the same:
- *Despite winning a scholarship, he could not afford to go to university.*

A Complete the second sentence so that it has a similar meaning to the first one. Use between two and five words, including the word given. Do not change the word given.

1 Although he was very old, he walked ten miles every day.   HIS
  Despite_____, he walked ten miles every day.
2 I studied hard. However, I did not pass the exam.   HARD
  Although _____, I did not pass the exam.
3 It was a holiday, but Tommy cycled to school as usual.   FACT
  In spite _____ it was a holiday, Tommy cycled to school as usual.
4 I'm sure I told her to stay at home, but she's gone out.   THOUGH
  Even _____stay at home, she's gone out.
5 Gerald did well in the competition, but he didn't win.   DOING
  Despite _____ in the competition, Gerald didn't win.

Other useful conjunctions are **to, in order to,** (expressing purpose), **and** (which links clauses of equal importance), **because, as, since** (used to give reasons), **when, as, since** (referring to time), **if, unless** (used in Conditionals – see **Unit 6**), and **so/such ... that** (expressing result):
- *As it was my turn, I paid for the drinks.* • *He's been ill since he arrived.*

In case does not mean **if**. It refers to the possibility of something happening. Use either a Present or Past tense after it. Do not use **will**:
- *Take a key in case the door is locked.* (It is possible the door will be locked.)
- *I didn't offer to help in case I offended him.* (I might have offended him.)

It's time is used to say that something should be done because the time to do it has come. It is not used with future tenses. There are two ways of using it, with the same meaning:
- *It's time for us to go home.* • *It's time we went home.*

B Complete the sentences with the correct form of the verb in brackets.

1 Otto's going to take sandwiches with him in case he _____ hungry.   (get)

2 Take an umbrella with you in case it _____ .   (rain)

3 Mark took out holiday insurance in case something _____ wrong.   (go)

4 I've reserved a table for them in case they _____ .   (turn up)

5 The police helicopter was flying overhead in case he _____ to escape.   (try)

C Complete the second sentence so that it has a similar meaning to the first one. Use between two and five words, including the word given. Do not change the word given.

1 I really should go to bed now.   FOR

It's time _____ bed.

2 Bianca ought to do some work now.   SOME

It's time _____ work.

3 At his age, he really should get married.   HE

It's high time _____ married.

4 We must say goodbye now.   SAY

It's time _____ goodbye.

5 You'd better post those letters as soon as possible.   POSTED

It's time _____ letters.

D Seven phrases or clauses have been removed from the following text.
Using your understanding of the text and your knowledge of conjunctions, choose from A-H the best phrase or clause to fill each gap. There is one more than you need.

François Truffaut (1932-1984) is one of France's best-known film directors. His work can be seen as an attempt to create a new cultural identity in the postwar period. He grew up in Pigalle, a lively cosmopolitan area in Paris and, 1) _____ , he always felt they neglected him. It was 2) _____ that he developed a great love for reading. He often played truant from school 3) _____ , and he kept careful notes on everything he saw. From 1945 onwards, cinema clubs started opening in Paris 4) _____ , and the directors Jean Renoir, Howard Hawks and Alfred Hitchcock became Truffaut's major influences. In the 1950s Truffaut became a film critic for an arts magazine, and later started making his own films. He believed strongly that directors must always follow their own artistic inspiration, 5) _____ , and put their personal stamp on their work. Truffaut and other young French directors, like Chabrol, Godard and Rohmer, became known as the New Wave, 6) _____ . Sadly, Truffaut's career was cut short in 1984, 7) _____ .

A   in order to go to the cinema

B   although his parents were not poor

C   when he died of brain cancer

D   and they produced many prize-winning films

E   because he was left on his own so much

F   but this was simply not possible at the time

G   despite pressure on them to make financially successful films

H   to show films that had previously been banned

Modal Verbs

> **Will, would, shall, should, can, could, may, might, must** and **ought to** are called modal verbs, and are very common in English. They do not have other forms (for the past or future), and do not use **do/did** to make a question or negative:
> * *Can you help me?* • *You mustn't do it.* • *I couldn't stop crying.*
>
> Note the short forms: **will not ~ won't, shall not ~ shan't, cannot ~ can't.**
>
> All these verbs except **ought to** take the infinitive without **to**:
> * *You must stay.* • *They can't come.* • *We won't see him.*
>
> Instead of **can**, you can use **be able to** in all tenses:
> * *I'll be able to get my visa later.* • *He was able to marry her after all.*
>
> Instead of **must**, you can use **have to** in all tenses:
> * *He had to be punished.* • *It's all right, you won't have to say anything.*

A Complete the sentences with *may, should, ought, must, have, can, be able.*

1 Oh no! My boss says I'll _____ to do overtime all this week!

2 I really think you _____ go and see the doctor, but it's up to you.

3 Joy _____ take early retirement this year. She hasn't decided yet.

4 There's no question about it. You _____ enter the competition. I'm sure you'll win!

5 Nicola _____ to take her studies more seriously in future.

6 Don't worry, I _____ help you with the typing, if you like.

7 Will Alex really _____ to finish the project by Friday?

B Match the two halves of the sentences correctly.

1 I'm afraid I won't be   A to fill in a form?

2 All staff must   B able to come.

3 Should I   C spare?

4 How much time can you   D follow the instructions.

5 Did you have   E give her a copy?

> **You mustn't** is a negative imperative, similar to **Don't**:
> * *You mustn't play football in the road. It's dangerous.*
>
> **You needn't** means the same as **you don't have to, it isn't necessary**:
> * *You needn't come to supper if you don't want to.*
>
> **Mustn't** and **needn't** are often used with **you**, but can be used with other pronouns, nouns and names:
> * *Andrew mustn't use the car without permission.*

C Complete the sentences with *mustn't* or *needn't.*

1 It says No Smoking. You _____ smoke here.

2 I don't think it will rain. David _____ take an umbrella.

3 I can manage, thanks. You _____ help me.

4 You _____ make so much noise. The baby's asleep.

5 You _____ shout at me. I'm not deaf!

Modal verbs are often used when we suppose that something is or isn't true, taking into account all the facts available.

Must is used when we assume something is true:
- *You haven't eaten all day. You must be hungry.*
- *She must love him. She's waited ten years to marry him.*

Can't is used when we suppose something is impossible:
- *Those results can't be right. You must have made a mistake.*

May/might are used when something is possible, but we are not sure about it:
- *Janice may be here. I'm not sure.* • *He might be able to help, but I can't promise.*

Note what happens if we are referring to something in the past:
- *He must have got the job.* • *You can't have lost your passport.*
- *They might have signed the form already.*

D Complete the sentences, using *must, can't, may* or *might* and the correct form of the verb in brackets.

1 She _____ English. Her Greek is too fluent! (be)

2 I can't find my keys. I _____ them in the car. (leave)

3 Why don't you rest for a while? You _____ tired after your long journey. (be)

4 She _____ his wife, but she looks too young. (be)

5 That new dress _____ her a fortune! (cost)

6 Your name's not on the register. You _____ this course! (book)

7 I suppose I _____ a mistake, but I'm almost sure I didn't. (make)

8 You _____ Helga's brother. She's told me all about you. (be)

Could is used to express possibility in a similar way to **may/might**:
- *This could be the house we're looking for.*

Could is also used to express general ability in the past:
- *She could swim when she was five.*

Was able to/managed to/succeeded in are used for a particular achievement in the past:
- *They all managed to pass the entry test.*

Couldn't can be used for both general and particular situations.

E Correct the sentences if necessary. Tick any which are already correct.

1 I could climb right to the top of the mountain that day.

2 Did you manage finishing your report?

3 We couldn't hear what the lecturer was saying.

4 Fortunately the firemen could put out the fire.

5 The pupils succeeded to collect enough money to buy a class computer.

6 Were you able to persuade him to go with you?

7 The newspapers couldn't be delivered on time.

8 The old lady could see the island from her window.

Adjectives

Adjectives describe nouns or pronouns. Common endings are **-ive, -ful, -less, -ic, -al, -able, -y**:
- *active, helpful, hopeless, artistic, practical, washable, angry*

Adjectives are not normally used to describe verbs, but **appear, feel, look, seem, smell, sound, taste** take an adjective, not an adverb, when the subject of the verb is being described:
- *The weather seemed perfect.* • *Your idea sounds great!* • *She looks happy!*

But note:
- *I tasted the risotto carefully.* • *He looked miserably at his work.*

Be always takes an adjective, not an adverb:
- *He's always very happy* • *Why is Helena so miserable?*

Notice the difference between adjectives ending in **-ing** and **-ed**:
- *a fascinating story* • *an interesting idea* • *He was fascinated.* • *I am puzzled.*

A Complete the text with adjectives made from the nouns given in capitals.

Young people today hope that, by gaining 1) _____ or 2) _____ qualifications from colleges and universities they will be able to get good jobs. But it is 3) _____ whether the 4) _____ world will be able to fit in so many 5) _____ young graduates, even if they are 6) _____ in their studies. Those who have 7) _____ training and some work experience, or 8) _____ contacts with the company of their choice, may be 9) _____ , but a large proportion of graduates will face a future of 10) _____ job-hunting and, sadly, 11) _____ income.

PROFESSION
PRACTICE
DOUBT
COMMERCE
HOPE/SUCCESS
SCIENCE
PERSON
LUCK
END
VARIETY

B Complete each sentence with the correct word from the pair in brackets.

1 Evie looked (angry/angrily) at her mother.
2 I'm feeling quite (comfortable/comfortably) now, thank you.
3 Your casserole smells (wonderful/wonderfully).
4 You'd do it more (easy/easily) if you took your time.
5 The presenter tasted the mixture (thoughtful/thoughtfully).
6 Julio seems rather (sad/sadly) today.
7 The burglar felt his way (careful/carefully) across the roof.
8 The new traffic scheme sounds (excellent/excellently).

C Complete the sentences by finding the correct adjective form of the verb in brackets.

1 He's always (amuse) by Charlie Chaplin films.
2 I thought the party was rather (bore).
3 The experience was absolutely (terrify).
4 We were (disgust) by Georgia's comments.
5 Stephen was (frighten) by the mysterious phone call.
6 Our holiday in Alaska was (thrill).
7 Susan is extremely (interest) in history.

Adverbs

> **Adverbs** are used to describe verbs (for verbs which take adjectives instead, see **Unit 28**):
> • *I thanked him politely and walked quickly away.* • *She laughed happily.*
> and also to describe or qualify adjectives:
> • *The plan was beautifully simple.*
>
> Most adverbs are formed by adding **-ly** to an adjective, or **-ally** after **-ic**:
> • *slow ~ slowly, graceful ~ gracefully* • *scientific ~ scientifically*
>
> Note that **hardly** is used negatively, with a different meaning from the adverb **hard**:
> • *He asked the girl out although he hardly knew her.*
>
> **Time adverbs** normally go right at the beginning or end of the clause:
> • *Last week we visited the museum.* • *She'll be there tomorrow.*
>
> **Adverbs of frequency**, e.g. *always, never, sometimes, often*, usually go between
> the subject and the verb: • *I never drink coffee.* • *They rarely go on holiday.*
> or between the two parts of a verb: • *She has always been helpful.*
>
> **Long adverbs** or **adverb phrases** usually go at the end of the clause:
> • *We get on extremely well.* • *He explained the plan in detail.*

A Complete the text with adverbs made from the adjectives given in capitals.

My uncle's firm of solicitors had a wonderful receptionist called Olive. She always arrived 1) _____ , 2) _____ dressed in a suit, and left the office 3) _____ , when all the work was done. Nobody worked as 4) _____ as Olive. She handled clients' calls both 5) _____ and extremely 6) _____ , while helping with the business correspondence. Although she was not 7) _____ qualified, she was 8) _____ skilled at drafting contracts. Olive's technique was to work 9) _____ but 10) _____ , and she was well known for her attention to detail. 11) _____ for my uncle and his partners, when Olive won the National Lottery, she 12) _____ decided to resign and travel the world in a gypsy caravan.

EARLY/ELEGANT
LATE
HARD
POLITE
EFFICIENT
LEGAL
HIGH
FAST
METHODICAL
UNFORTUNATE
SUDDEN

B Correct the following sentences, if necessary. Tick any which are already correct.

1 I go often to the cinema in the afternoon.
2 We do every day our homework.
3 I like very much melon and strawberries.
4 Andreas drove as fast as possible the car.
5 Caroline would sometimes practise her guitar in the bathroom.
6 The police entered suddenly the house.
7 The students passed with a Grade C the exam.
8 The grass occasionally was cut by a neighbour.
9 They always have attended this school.
10 Yesterday he got up late.

Recycling

A Eight phrases or clauses have been removed from the following text. Using your understanding of the text and your knowledge of grammar, choose from A-I the best phrase or clause to fill each gap. There is one more than you need.

In 1995 the British woman Alison Hargreaves became the first female climber to conquer Mount Everest, 1) _____ , without oxygen or the help of sherpas, the native Nepalese 2) _____ . Only one other person had achieved this before – Reinhold Messner, 3) _____ .

Ms Hargreaves had spent over a year 4) _____ by training on the Scottish mountain Ben Nevis, 5) _____ . She was confident she would reach the summit, 6) _____ because of bad weather. Mr Ballard said 7) _____ , and very proud of her, 8) _____ .

Tragically, Alison Hargreaves fell to her death a few months later, in an avalanche on K2, the world's second highest peak.

A despite being forced to give up the previous year's attempt
B where her husband Jim Ballard worked part-time
C who normally carry climbers' equipment and supplies
D although they had never really doubted she would manage it
E preparing for the trip
F who reached the top in 1980
G the highest mountain in the world
H but he had hoped the weather would improve
I that he and their children were delighted

B Complete the second sentence so that it has a similar meaning to the first one. Use between two and five words, including the word given. Do not change the word given.

1 I don't think I can do the work in time.   ABLE
   I'm afraid I _____ do the work in time.
2 Did they make you sign the contract?   TO
   Did you _____ the contract?
3 I really think you should take him to hospital.   OUGHT
   In my opinion you _____ to hospital.
4 When Hugh was younger, he often played football.   PLAY
   Hugh _____ football when he was younger.
5 I'm not sure whether Pablo will be there or not.   NOT
   Pablo _____ there.
6 Don't be so rude to people!   MUSTN'T
   You_____ to people.
7 I think you should have the pool cleaned.   CLEANING
   I think _____ .
8 Don't bother to lock the door.   NEEDN'T
   You _____ the door.

C Complete the passage, using one word for each space.

The Lake District, in 1) _____ north-west of England, is one of the 2) _____ popular areas in Britain for tourists to visit. 3) _____ only about 40,000 people live there all year round, 4) _____ are about 14 million visitors every year. The area 5) _____ declared a national park some time ago, and is managed 6) _____ Cumbria County Council and the National Park Authority.

These bodies are now seriously worried 7) _____ the effect of the large influx of tourists on the area. Footpaths 8) _____ repairing, 9) _____ they are used by increasing numbers of walkers. Some narrow country lanes are 10) _____ suitable for the summer rush of cars, caravans and coaches. There are local complaints 11) _____ the authorities are 12) _____ interested 13) _____ the needs of tourists than of residents.

For several months officials have been discussing 14) _____ and other problems, and they now feel it is 15) _____ to make some changes. In their plans, 16) _____ published, they suggest that some minor roads 17) _____ be closed to traffic. They also want 18) _____ public transport, with 19) _____ fares than at present. It is hoped that this scheme 20) _____ be acceptable to all, and will improve life for everybody in the Lake District.

D Complete the text by making an adjective or adverb from each word given in capitals.

Start an 1) _____ new career today!
Learn how to edit and proof-read 2) _____
and 3) _____ , on our certificated four-day
courses. Our team of 4) _____ experienced
5) _____ tutors will help you to acquire the
6) _____ skills which will open doors for you.
Our courses are 7) _____ , and will offer you
the chance to learn and practise on a 8) _____
basis. Correspondence courses are also 9) _____
worldwide. And the price is 10) _____ low!
Does all this sound 11) _____ to you? Well, if
you are 12) _____ , give us a ring or drop us a line
13) _____ , to ask for your sample pack and
application form.

EXCITE
ACCURACY
SPEED
HIGH
ENTHUSIASM
PROFESSION
RESIDENCE
DAY
AVAIL
INCREDIBLE
ATTRACT
INTEREST
IMMEDIATE

UNIT 31

Phrasal Verbs with Look

look after	look at	look for	look into
look like	look on	look out	look round
look through	look up	look down on	look forward to
look up to			

Remember – some phrasal verbs have more than one meaning.

A Complete the sentences with the correct form of a phrasal verb with **look**.

1 _____! There's a bus coming!
2 The police are _____ the robbery.
3 She _____ the room, but couldn't see her sister anywhere.
4 I'm _____ my pen. Have you seen it?
5 I'll have to _____ her report again in more detail before the meeting.
6 If you can't remember his phone number, you can always _____ it _____ in the phone book.
7 He _____ exactly _____ his brother. I think they must be twins.
8 Alan wasn't _____ his textbook. He was just staring out of the window.
9 She was very proud of her qualifications, and _____ people she thought were uneducated.
10 I'm really _____ the party next week.
11 The crowd _____ , as the two men continued fighting.
12 Margarita never got married. She spent most of her life _____ her invalid mother.

B Complete the second sentence so that it has a similar meaning to the first one. Use between two and five words, including the word given. Do not change the word given.

1 He has always respected and admired his professor.   TO
He has always _____ his professor.
2 Athina resembles her sister: they are both tall and slim.   LIKE
Athina _____ her sister: they are both tall and slim.
3 Can you look after my cat while I'm on holiday?   CARE
Can you _____ my cat while I'm on holiday?
4 I'll have to try and find a flat in Rome.   LOOK
I'll have to _____ a flat in Rome.
5 Martin didn't think much of his cousin's achievements.   ON
Martin _____ his cousin's achievements.

C Fill the spaces with the correct particle(s), e.g. *over*.

1 look ____   a difficult word   a phone number   a friend
2 look ____   a problem   a theft   the matter
3 look ____   small children   a pet   your parents if they're old or ill
4 look ____   the view   the blackboard   the signpost
5 look ____   a lost book   a new flat   an aim in life

Phrasal Verbs with Take

take after	take away	take back	take down	take in
take off	take on	take out	take over	take up

Remember – some phrasal verbs have more than one meaning.

A Complete the sentences with the correct form of a phrasal verb with **take**.

1 The plane _____ at 3.30 p.m. today.

2 Are you _____ your girlfriend _____ tonight?

3 The secretary _____ the information her boss was dictating.

4 Jonathan _____ his father, you know. They are both very intelligent.

5 When Tom retires, he's going to _____ golf.

6 I'm sorry I offended you. I _____ what I said.

7 The electronics company failed to make a profit and was eventually _____ by a larger one.

8 I've explained it to him four times, but he just doesn't seem to _____ it _____.

9 Because of an increase in orders, the factory manager _____ a hundred new workers.

10 How many library books can I _____ with this ticket?

11 I don't want ice-cream all over my clothes. _____ it _____!

12 I know the dress is too long, but we can easily _____ it _____.

B Match each phrase or clause with the best ending. Write the letter next to the number on the right.

Now do the same for the rest of the exercise.

1 The policewoman took	A off his boss very well.	1 ___
2 Your friend takes	B down my statement in her notebook as I was speaking.	2 ___
3 At the time I was taken	C back his criticism.	3 ___
4 He should apologize and take	D in by his story, which I realized later was untrue.	4 ___
5 Singapore Plastics are taking	E after their mother, you know.	5 ___
6 The twins take	F off in thick fog yesterday.	6 ___
7 The helicopter had to take	G up tennis again, at the local club.	7 ___
8 When I have time, I'll take	H on 200 skilled workers for this year's export drive.	8 ___

C Fill the spaces with the correct particle, e.g. *down*.

1 take ____   your clothes   in fog   a famous person

2 take ____   information   a lodger   someone who trusts you

3 take ____   tennis   a pair of trousers   a suggestion

4 take ____   a new job   extra work   more staff

5 take ____   the shirt to the shop   the library books   what you said

Phrasal Verbs with Put

put away	put down	put forward	put in
put off	put on	put out	put through
put someone up	put up with		

Remember – some phrasal verbs have more than one meaning.

A Complete the sentences with the correct form of a phrasal verb with **put**.

1 The firemen only just managed to _____ the fire _____.
2 I'm sorry, I can't _____ his behaviour any longer.
3 The house is much warmer now that we've _____ central heating.
4 If your friend is ill, you'll have to _____ your holiday. You can go to France later in the year.
5 Hello, are you still there? I'm _____ you _____ to Mr Jones now.
6 I've _____ so much weight recently that I'll have to go on a diet.
7 He has _____ a deposit on a car, and he'll pay the rest later.
8 I can _____ you _____ for the night, but you'll be in a sleeping-bag on the floor, I'm afraid!
9 I've never seen such an untidy room! _____ your things _____ at once!
10 I would like to _____ a new proposal.
11 Hurry up! It doesn't matter which shoes you _____! We're late!
12 The restaurant was so dirty that I was quite _____ eating there.

B Underline the correct word or phrase to complete each sentence.

1 Last month William *put up Tim / put Tim up* for a few nights.
2 A new theatre company *is putting on / is putting up with* Hamlet this week at the Civic Centre.
3 I'd like to *put off / put on* my flight until next week.
4 Please *put down / put out* all cigarettes and fasten your seat belts.
5 I simply can't agree to the plan you're *putting forward / putting out*.
6 Sorry to keep you waiting. I'm *putting you over / putting you through* to the Manager now.
7 Henry has been *putting on / putting in* a lot of overtime recently.
8 They *put away / put off* the tent until the following summer.
9 I'm afraid there isn't a quieter room. You'll just have to *put up with / put up* this one.
10 I wanted a new stereo, but the prices in the shops were so high that I was rather *put out / put off*.

C Fill the spaces with the correct particle(s), e.g. *in*.

1 put ____   a journey   doing homework   telling him
2 put ____   the book   the riot   a deposit
3 put ____   a coat   three kilos   the light
4 put ____   the rubbish to be collected   a hand to help someone   your cigarette
5 put ____   prices   a notice   with her rudeness

Phrasal Verbs with Bring

bring about	bring back	bring down	bring in
bring on	bring out	bring round	bring up

Remember – some phrasal verbs have more than one meaning.

A Complete the sentences with the correct form of a phrasal verb with **bring**.

1 When his mother died, Brendan was _____ by relatives in Australia.

2 I'm sure getting wet last week _____ my cold.

3 The publishers are _____ Tony's first novel in the spring.

4 She had fainted, but we managed to _____ her _____ by splashing water on her face.

5 Whenever I hear that tune, it _____ happy memories of my childhood.

6 Her part-time work _____ enough to pay the bills.

7 By lobbying Members of Parliament, we hope to _____ a change in the law.

8 When his customers refused to buy, the shopkeeper was forced to _____ his prices.

9 Could I _____ one last point, Mr Chairman?

10 Parliament has just _____ a new law to protect rare birds.

11 I hope I'll be able to _____ him _____ to my point of view before we vote on it.

12 In the end the government was _____ by a crisis in the Cabinet.

B Match each phrase or clause with the best ending. Write the letter next to the number on the right.

1 The enemy plane   A doesn't bring in much money.   1 ____

2 That's the same point   B was brought up by my grandparents.   2 ____

3 That kind of job   C you brought up earlier in the meeting.   3 ____

4 The news of his wife's accident   D was brought down over the desert.   4 ____

5 After I was five I   E brought on a heart attack.   5 ____

Now do the same for the rest of the exercise.

6 His detailed report brought about   F your photo album when you come.   6 ____

7 She brought him round   G such an unpopular law.   7 ____

8 He asked his secretary to bring in   H a change in company policy.   8 ____

9 Perhaps you could bring round   I to her way of thinking.   9 ____

10 I think the government will regret bringing in   J the next client.   10 ____

Phrasal Verbs with Set, Stand and Run

set back	set down	set in	set off	set out
set up	stand by	stand for	stand in	stand out
stand up to	run across	run away	run down	run out
run over	run up			

Remember – some phrasal verbs have more than one meaning.

A Match each phrasal verb with the correct definition. (Other definitions may be possible.)

1 stand for   A meet by chance
2 run out   B represent
3 run over   C write on paper, as a record
4 set down   D support or be loyal to
5 set back   E prevent progress
6 stand by   F have no more
7 run across   G arrange or show
8 set out   H knock down (someone with a car)
9 stand in   I act as a substitute
10 stand up to   J resist or confront

B Complete the passage, using one word for each space.

What's on at the cinema?

One film 1) _____ out this week from the rest – the beautifully acted *Journey to the Outback*, in which Sandra, played by Denise Jacobs, 2) _____ off on a journey across Australia to find her roots and, eventually, happiness. But if you don't like happy endings, then you should see *Dr Roberts*, the tragic tale of a young woman doctor who 3) _____ up her own practice in a remote village. Although she's bright and good at her job, she isn't tough enough to 4) _____ up to the villagers' rejection of her and her lifestyle. I won't tell you what happens in the end, but there wasn't a dry eye in the house when I saw it!

Another film worth seeing is *Don't Tell Daddy*, a light comedy involving a likeable teenager, Matt, who 5) _____ up huge bills on his father's credit card, and then has to discover a way of paying the debts before Daddy finds out. He finally decides to run 6) _____ to sea, in order to make some money. Tom Gish, who plays Matt, gives an excellent performance, and there are some very amusing moments. One film I wouldn't recommend is *Boston Baby*, about an elderly couple living in New England, just as winter is 7) _____ in. There's very little plot or anything else in this and, while I never like to run 8) _____ a director's first effort, I do feel three hours is much too long for this tedious, slow-moving story.

C Match each phrasal verb with the best phrase. Do not use any item more than once. Write the letter next to the number on the right.

1 set up	A of bottled water	1 ____
2 stand in	B an office in Oxford	2 ____
3 run out	C from the others	3 ____
4 stand out	D a friend unexpectedly	4 ____
5 run across	E at the dress rehearsal	5 ____

UNIT 36

Recycling

A Decide whether the following sentences are true or false. Write T or F beside them.

1 If you've lost your book, you look after it.
2 If you admire someone, you look up to him or her.
3 Cold water helps to bring back someone who has fainted.
4 If you want your friend to join in the discussion, you bring him on.
5 If you put off a meeting, you've decided not to hold it at all.
6 If you weigh more than usual, you've put on weight.
7 In order to keep warm, you should take on more clothes.
8 If you take down the information, you can refer to it later.

B Choose the correct word or phrase to complete each sentence. Write the letter in the space.

1 No matter how often I explain it, he doesn't seem to _____.
   a) put it through   b) take it in   c) take it on   d) put it in
2 That is the proposal which I shall _____ to the Managing Director.
   a) put forward   b) take down   c) bring up   d) put on
3 She's a very good child. She always _____ her toys.
   a) puts up   b) takes down   c) brings on   d) puts away
4 It's getting dark. Please _____ the lights on.
   a) take   b) bring   c) put   d) set
5 Leila _____ the information she wanted in her reference books.
   a) looked after   b) looked up   c) took out   d) took up
6 Local shopkeepers are _____ their prices for the summer sales.
   a) taking down   b) looking on   c) taking off   d) bringing down

C Underline the correct word or phrase to complete each sentence.

1 She *takes after / looks like* her friend Anna: they're both very dark.
2 We can *look / put* Ahmed up when we visit Tunis.
3 I've got just enough money to *bring / put* down a deposit.
4 Have the dustmen *taken away / put up* the rubbish?
5 Sarah *brought / put* up an interesting point at the meeting.
6 That lorry's coming towards us! Look *up / out*!

D Match each phrasal verb with the best phrase. Do not use any item more than once. Write the letter next to the number on the right.

1 look down on	A a child	1 ____
2 bring up	B a play	2 ____
3 put on	C more workers	3 ____
4 take on	D a new hobby	4 ____
5 take up	E other people	5 ____

Now do the same for the rest of the exercise.

6 take over	F a fire	6 ____
7 put out	G a new bathroom	7 ____
8 bring in	H another company	8 ____
9 take back	I a good salary	9 ____
10 put in	J what you said	10 ____

E Complete the passage, using one word for each space.

Look 1) _____ ! Asthma's about!

Asthma is a disease which literally 2) _____ the breath away. It does this regularly to three million sufferers in Britain, and it is on the increase all over the world. Apparently it is 3) _____ on by things like chest infections, the weather, cigarette smoke and common allergies. If you look it 4) _____ in a dictionary, the usual definition given is 'a respiratory disorder'. But nobody knows exactly why asthma occurs. Scientists have put 5) _____ years of research 6) _____ into the possible causes of asthma, but have produced no conclusive results. The Ancient Greeks, Egyptians, Chinese and Indians all mentioned asthma in their writings, and put 7) _____ suggestions for treatment. Researchers these days are looking 8) _____ different groups of asthma patients – rich and poor, children and adults, office-workers and country people – and they say that the disease is spreading, even to areas where previously it did not exist. Fortunately, asthma is treatable, but experts still need to find a method of prevention. While they are looking 9) _____ a solution to this problem, we sufferers will just have to 10) _____ up with it, and look 11) _____ to the day when this unpleasant disease can be wiped out.

F Read the text and decide which word (A, B, C or D) best fits each space.

Next time you have to put 1) _____ a picnic because of pouring rain, or take the dog 2) _____ in the freezing cold, don't blame the weatherman. It's not his or her fault that the weather isn't perfect all the time. This is the kind of thing you often hear people say, in shops and offices and at bus stops:

'It was the rain all last week that 3) _____ on my cold.'

'Would you believe it? It's August and I'm 4) _____ on another pullover!'

'Perhaps it's winter 5) _____ in already!'

'I don't know why we 6) _____ up with it. I'm seriously considering moving to Florida!'

'Have you played any tennis recently?' 'Not a chance, it's been too wet. I think I'd better 7) _____ up a nice indoor game like chess next summer!'

Most people take bad weather as a personal insult, and become quite annoyed about it. If they 8) _____ out on a trip, the weather is the main topic of conversation, until they run 9) _____ of things to say about it. Just remember that the weatherman probably feels the same as you do about it!

	A	B	C	D
1	on	off	over	about
2	out	away	off	into
3	set	came	brought	put
4	putting	taking	bringing	getting
5	setting	putting	standing	running
6	look	take	stand	put
7	look	bring	take	set
8	set	take	run	look
9	away	out	down	across

Phrasal Verbs with Come

come across	come back	come down	come in
come into	come off	come on	come out
come round	come to	come up	come down with
come up with			

Remember – some phrasal verbs have more than one meaning.

A Complete the sentences with the correct form of a phrasal verb with **come**.

1 When I was tidying up my wardrobe, I _____ this old hat.
2 Barbara Cathcart's latest novel _____ last week.
3 My uncle, who was in India last year, has _____ a bad attack of malaria.
4 Your bill _____ £24.50, madam. Thank you.
5 The scientist _____ a brilliant solution to the problem.
6 I'm sorry I can't meet you for lunch after all. Something important has _____.
7 When she _____ after the operation, she immediately asked for her husband.
8 He worked hard on the scheme, but it never really _____.
9 House prices _____ during the recession, and have not gone up again yet.
10 We can catch the train if we run! _____!
11 I'm ready for you now. Push open the door and _____.
12 When Uncle Tim emigrated to Australia twenty years ago, we never thought he would _____.
13 When Nadia's grandfather died, she _____ all his money.
14 One of your coat buttons has _____.
15 At first he didn't agree with me, but he soon _____.

B Match each phrase or clause with the best ending. Write the letter next to the number on the right.

1 He came across   A flu last week.   1 ____
2 She came down with   B after five years in Japan.   2 ____
3 He came round   C a valuable document in the library.   3 ____
4 Chris came back   D an unexpected inheritance.   4 ____
5 Anne came into   E after lying unconscious for a while.   5 ____

Now do the same for the rest of the exercise.

6 The plan he proposed   F are coming on well.   6 ____
7 I don't think these coffee stains   G but she came round in the end.   7 ____
8 She was against the idea at first   H never came off.   8 ____
9 Those roses of yours   I because something has come up.   9 ____
10 I'm in a hurry   J will come out.   10 ____

Phrasal Verbs with Go

go away	go by	go down	go for
go into	go off	go on	go out
go over	go through	go up	go with

Remember – some phrasal verbs have more than one meaning.

A Complete the sentences with the correct form of a phrasal verb with **go**.

1 People get older as the years _____.

2 His first speech _____ very well and everybody clapped.

3 I think he's broken his leg. I'll stay with him while you _____ help.

4 When I finish my studies, I'll probably _____ teaching.

5 Leave me alone! Just _____!

6 As we sat there, the lights suddenly _____, plunging the house into darkness.

7 If you're _____ tonight, Elaine, remember to take your door key with you.

8 Just imagine what the poor man _____, locked up for a crime he hadn't committed.

9 That meat smells terrible! I think it has _____.

10 The rate of inflation _____ last year from 4% to 5%.

11 I'm afraid those red curtains don't _____ the green carpet.

12 He stopped for a drink of water, and then _____ to finish his speech.

13 Angrily the teacher asked what was _____.

14 Did you understand that, or shall I _____ it again?

15 I'm sure you can do it. _____ ! Just try!

B Match each phrase or clause with the best ending. Write the letter next to the number on the right.

1	The building was attacked and	A	go off at midnight.	1 ____
2	House prices in this area	B	went through all his pockets.	2 ____
3	He didn't find the keys although he	C	went up in flames.	3 ____
4	I told you not to	D	went down last year.	4 ____
5	The bomb was timed to	E	let the fire go out.	5 ____

Now do the same for the rest of the exercise.

6	He goes through	F	a cup of coffee now.	6 ____
7	She went on talking	G	to sleep immediately	7 ____
8	Let's go for	H	and we never saw her again.	8 ____
9	The children went off	I	despite the interruptions.	9 ____
10	She went away	J	six pairs of shoes a year.	10 ____

Phrasal Verbs with Get

get away	get by	get in	get off	get on
get out	get over	get round	get through	get up
get away with	get on with	get out of	get round to	

Remember – some phrasal verbs have more than one meaning.

A Complete the sentences with the correct form of a phrasal verb with **get**.

1 Bruce made an excuse so that he could _____ doing his homework.

2 I'm catching a plane on Friday evening, so I'll need to _____ from the office earlier than usual.

3 How are the children _____ at school these days?

4 The door's locked. We can't _____ without a key.

5 They haven't got much money, but they manage to _____.

6 The prisoners must have _____ through that open window.

7 It takes some patients several months to _____ this type of operation.

8 'When are you going to answer that letter?' 'There's no hurry. I'll _____ it sometime this week.'

9 Did you _____ to your father on the phone?

10 What time do you usually _____ in the morning?

11 I was half asleep on the bus and forgot to _____ at my stop.

12 Don't talk! Just _____ your work! Hurry up!

B Complete the second sentence so that it has a similar meaning to the first one. Use between two and five words, including the word given. Do not change the word given.

1 I had a good relationship with my neighbours until last year. WELL
I _____ with my neighbours until last year.

2 The robbers escaped with £2 million in banknotes. AWAY
The robbers _____ £2 million in banknotes.

3 I simply can't make her understand. TO
I simply can't _____ her.

4 Malik never really recovered from the shock. GOT
Malik never really _____ the shock.

5 She's getting on a bit, isn't she? OLD
She's _____ , isn't she?

6 Sally sometimes pretends to be ill to avoid going to school. OUT
Sally sometimes pretends to be ill _____ going to school.

C Fill the spaces with the correct particle(s), e.g. *in*.

1 get ____   a bus   to sleep   a bike

2 get ____   all his homework   an exam   money fast

3 get ____   a problem   the rules   your father

4 get ____   a taxi   doing the housework   prison

5 get ____   an illness   a fence   your shyness

UNIT 40

Phrasal Verbs with Turn

turn against	turn away	turn back	turn down
turn into	turn off	turn on	turn out
turn over	turn to	turn up	

Remember – some phrasal verbs have more than one meaning.

A Complete the sentences with the correct form of a phrasal verb with **turn**.

1 Could you _____ your radio, please? It's far too loud.

2 I wasn't expecting Anne, but she _____ on the doorstep last night.

3 When Simone's parents died, she _____ her friends for support.

4 We were halfway to the airport, when we had to _____ for our passports, which we had left at home.

5 Because they were not smartly dressed, they were _____ from the nightclub.

6 Despite the bitter cold, a huge crowd _____ to greet the President.

7 There's more on the next page, so please _____.

8 Would you _____ the lights when you leave the room?

9 I didn't want to go to the wedding, so I _____ the invitation.

10 The maths teacher used to like me, but now he's _____ me.

11 That spoilt child has _____ a generous, unselfish girl.

12 As soon as the gardener _____ the water, the sprinklers started working.

B Match each phrase or clause with the best ending. Write the letter next to the number on the right.

Now do the same for the rest of the exercise.

1 In the end it turned	A out for the election tomorrow.	1 ____
2 The doorman turned	B out that few students wanted to attend the ceremony.	2 ____
3 You could have the ` trousers turned	C us away from the disco, because we couldn't prove we were over 18.	3 ____
4 I think lots of voters will turn	D up, if they're too long.	4 ____
5 My sister persuaded me to turn	E up under the sofa, where we hadn't thought of looking.	5 ____
6 The town has turned	F down the job they offered me in Geneva.	6 ____
7 Stella's bag finally turned	G back to shelter in a mountain hut.	7 ____
8 The weather was awful, so we turned	H into a smart holiday resort.	8 ____

C Fill the spaces with the correct particle, e.g. *back*.

1 turn ____   the road   the television   the tap

2 turn ____   a stone   the problem   the page

3 turn ____   your friends for help   a life of crime   ice

4 turn ____   an offer   the volume   your collar

5 turn ____   to vote   better than expected   1000 cars a week

Phrasal Verbs with See, Give and Break

see off	see through	see to	give away	give in
give out	give up	break away	break down	break in(to)
break off	break out	break out of	break through	break up

Remember – some phrasal verbs have more than one meaning.

A Match each phrasal verb with the correct definition. (Other definitions may be possible.)

1	give away	A	stop a habit (e.g. smoking)
2	see off	B	begin (war, fire, disease)
3	break out	C	donate, allow someone to have without paying
4	give out	D	arrange or organize
5	give up	E	understand that someone is deceiving you
6	see to	F	achieve success, make a discovery
7	break in	G	admit defeat
8	break off	H	end (a relationship, negotiations)
9	give in	I	escape, leave
10	break away	J	enter a house by force
11	break through	K	distribute
12	see through	L	say goodbye to someone (usually at a station or airport)

B Some of the lines in this letter are correct, and others have a word which should not be there. Tick any lines which are correct. Write down any words which should not be there.

As soon as school will breaks up for the summer, we set
always off on our annual trip to the coast. My mother has
given up to worrying about packing – we all just throw
whatever we need into the car and hope we have remembered
everything. To prevent anyone breaking in to, we lock the
house up carefully and tell to the neighbours we're going
away. My brother's young friends, who live next door, always
see of us off, and wave goodbye until we're out of sight. Last
year the car was broke down on the motorway, which meant a
long delay until someone could see to doing it. The year before,
there was a police road-block on our route – a convict had
broken away out of a high-security prison. It's often an
eventful trip! After we've been in the car for an hour, we're starving,
so Mum reluctantly gives us out the sandwiches, which we eat
immediately. Then we start demanding the ice-cream, until
finally she gives in us and we stop in a village to buy some.

1 □
2 □
3 □
4 □
5 □
6 □
7 □
8 □
9 □
10 □
11 □
12 □
13 □
14 □
15 □
16 □

C Match each phrasal verb with the best phrase. Do not use any item more than once. Write the letter next to the number on the right.

1	break into	A	eating three big meals a day	1 ____
2	give up	B	the star's mansion	2 ____
3	see through	C	diplomatic relations with the countries involved	3 ____
4	give away	D	someone's excuses	4 ____
5	break off	E	all his money to charity	5 ____

Recycling

A Decide whether the following sentences are true or false. Write T or F beside them.

1 Getting over an illness means recovering from it.
2 If you turn down an offer, you have accepted it.
3 People come into money by earning it day by day.
4 At a smart disco the doorman might turn you away if you're wearing beach clothes.
5 If you come across something, you didn't expect to find it.
6 Food which has gone off is still good to eat.
7 If you get round your father, you are inviting him to visit you.
8 You can ask the teacher to go over a difficult point again.

B Choose the correct phrase to complete each sentence. Write the letter in the space.

1 Lucia was surprised when her guests _____ late for the party.
   a) came up   b) turned up   c) looked up   d) put up
2 Sergio noticed how cold it was when he _____ the plane.
   a) got off   b) took off   c) went off   d) went out of
3 All the ideas were good, but Michael _____ the best plan of all.
   a) put on   b) got on with   c) came up   d) came up with
4 I think a plain blouse would _____ better _____ that skirt.
   a) go / with   b) put / with   c) come / with   d) go / to
5 She _____ the flat three times, before deciding to buy it.
   a) came round   b) brought round   c) looked round   d) got round
6 Although he's my friend, I find it hard to _____ his selfishness.
   a) get out of   b) come up with   c) take on   d) put up with

C Underline the correct word or phrase to complete each sentence.

1 Guy is looking *for / forward to* the barbecue at the weekend.
2 The kidnappers managed to *get / go* away with the ransom money.
3 I can't hear the news. Turn *up / off* the volume please.
4 Unfortunately Simon's new plan did not *come off / turn out*.
5 With a great roar the rocket *got / went* up.
6 His dry-cleaning bill *came / went* to almost £15.

D Match each phrasal verb with the best noun or noun phrase. Do not use any item more than once. Write the letter next to the number on the right.

1 turn against	A an illness	1 ____
2 go through	B a horse	2 ____
3 get off	C a difficult time	3 ____
4 take down	D somebody	4 ____
5 come down with	E a message	5 ____

Now do the same for the rest of the exercise.

6 take in	F a shock	6 ____
7 get on with	G the page	7 ____
8 turn over	H a phone call	8 ____
9 get over	I the instructions	9 ____
10 put through	J most people	10 ____

E Complete the passage, using one word for each space.

The Moscow metro system is over sixty years old. Sometimes called 'the people's underground palace', it has stood 1) _____ well to the passing of time. It carries nine million passengers a day at an average speed of 42 k.p.h., and now, even though it has 2) _____ out of money, it still offers impressive examples of past splendour. Tourists from all over the world come to look 3) _____ the stations lined with granite and marble and decorated with mosaics and chandeliers. Some of the names have changed: for example, Marx Prospekt has turned 4) _____ Hunter's Row. Some Muscovites find it hard to 5) _____ in the changes, but they are justly proud of their underground and want to 6) _____ after it. Recently a strike was threatened, to force the government to invest in the system. The plan came 7) _____ , and so a new line and new stations will be built.

The Moscow metro 8) _____ out among its international competitors for being almost completely free of advertising. Although that will change soon, transport managers have promised to see 9) _____ it that any advertising will be done tastefully. Wherever you go in the world, you won't come 10) _____ a grander or more impressive underground system. Whether you're a local, 11) _____ your friends off or travelling to work, or a tourist, visiting Moscow for the first time, spare a moment to appreciate the works of art all around you, before 12) _____ on with your journey.

F Read the text and decide which word (A, B, C or D) best fits each space.

Looking 1) _____ a property abroad? A holiday home or a future investment? We think we can come 2) _____ with just the sort of thing you want. Let us at Dream Homes Limited answer a few of your questions. *Which area?* Our experts can 3) _____ forward a number of suggestions for you to go 4) _____ and choose from. *What kind of place should I buy?* You could buy a smart town-centre apartment, if you like action and nightlife. Or why not 5) _____ away from it all and opt for a cottage in the heart of the country? *Will there be problems?* We have years of experience in this field. Our staff can 6) _____ round any difficulties, and will make the whole process as easy as possible for you. *How much will it cost?* You won't have to rob a bank, sell the car or even give 7) _____ smoking to be able to afford it! Recently, overseas house prices have gone 8) _____ slightly, so this is the perfect moment to buy. *Will it be legal?* All the details of the sale and purchase will be set 9) _____ in a contract, which is carefully checked by our legal team. *What's my next step?* 10) _____ round and see us sometime! Or give us a ring on 01350-750804.

	A	B	C	D
1	after	for	at	into
2	up	over	out	in
3	look	come	put	take
4	in	through	for	across
5	bring	stand	go	get
6	come	bring	get	take
7	up	in	away	out
8	down	up	off	away
9	up	in	off	down
10	Bring	Come	Go	Get

Work

A Complete the passage with some of these words. Do not use any word or phrase more than once.

> applicants application employer promotion
> interview vacancies employment curriculum vitae
> salary experience unemployed post
> employees training Personnel Manager

There are several things to remember if you are applying for a new job. Most companies advertise their 1) _____ in the newspapers, and there are normally a lot of 2) _____ for each 3) _____. A good letter of 4) _____ is therefore very important. You should enclose with it your 5) _____, so that the 6) _____ knows about your qualifications and 7) _____. If you are applying to a large company, address your letter to the 8) _____, who deals with appointing new staff. If you are invited to an 9) _____, make sure you arrive suitably dressed and on time. Remember to ask politely about 10) _____ prospects, as well as further 11) _____, and last but not least, the 12) _____ and holiday arrangements.

B Match each occupation with a place of work. Write the correct letter next to the number on the right.

1 surgeon	A court	1 ____
2 bricklayer	B surgery	2 ____
3 cashier	C studio	3 ____
4 artist	D operating theatre	4 ____
5 mechanic	E building site	5 ____
6 doctor	F bank	6 ____
7 barrister	G salon	7 ____
8 hairdresser	H garage	8 ____

C Choose the correct word from the pair in brackets to complete the sentences.

1 Pepe is leaving the company. He's going to _____ because he's found a better job. (retire/resign)

2 I've heard the boss is going to _____ him soon. (sack/resign)

3 It's a good idea for employees to join the company _____ scheme if they can. (pension/rent)

4 Sarah was made _____ recently, but soon managed to find another teaching _____. (bankrupt/redundant, work/job)

5 Most qualified people are paid a reasonable _____. (pay/salary)

D Answer these questions as fully as you can, in conversation or in writing.

1 Do you live to work, or work to live?

2 Describe your ideal job.

3 Is job satisfaction more important to you than a high salary?

4 Would you go to a different town or country to work if necessary?

5 Do you think running a home and bringing up children can be called a job?

Education

A Complete the passage with some of these words. Do not use any word more than once.

primary	secondary	compulsory	marks
reports	fees	exams	private	state
	discipline	boarding	term	

In countries where parents are legally obliged to make sure their children receive a satisfactory education, school is 1) _____ for all children. Pupils usually attend 2) _____ school up to the age of 11 or 12. Then they move on to 3) _____ school, where they stay for the next five years or so. Most schools have 4) _____ at the end of the year to test pupils' progress. If pupils' 5) _____ are not good enough, they may have to do extra work to catch up, and in some countries they repeat the school year. Teachers write 6) _____ about their pupils, and these can be discussed with parents. Most pupils attend 7) _____ schools, which are free. However, some parents send their children to 8) _____ schools, where the 9) _____ may be quite high. If parents work abroad, they may send their children to a 10) _____ school, where pupils live for up to three months at a time. Boarders at these schools usually only go home at the end of each 11) _____.

B In the same way as above, use these words to complete the passage.

university	subject	graduate	studies	degree
education	career	training	lecture	grant

When you've finished the compulsory part of your 1) _____, you then have to decide what to do next. You could leave school to find a job straightaway, you could undergo 2) _____ for a specific 3) _____, or you may decide to continue your 4) _____ in order to enter 5) _____. If you go to university, you will have to work hard at your chosen 6) _____, in order to qualify for your 7) _____. If you are lucky, your government may give you a 8) _____ to help you pay your living expenses. Even when you have completed your studies, and are a university 9) _____, you may have difficulty in finding the right job.

C Answer these questions as fully as you can, in conversation or in writing.

1 Which do you think provides a better education, a state school or a private school?
2 Should pupils have to wear school uniform?
3 What is the point of going to school?
4 What are the advantages and disadvantages of teaching as a career?
5 Would you like to go/have gone to a boarding school?

The Environment

A Complete the passage with some of these words. Do not use any word or phrase more than once.

ecological	ozone	developing countries	acid rain
chemicals	rainforests	die out	in the wild	climate
habitats	resources	renewable	pollution
planet	in captivity	endangered species

Many environmental experts are pessimistic about the future of our
1) _____. They say that in the next few years harmful 2) _____
will further damage the 3) _____ layer, there will be more losses of
irreplaceable tropical 4) _____, and serious air 5) _____ will
cause the 6) _____ itself to change. They also warn us that Third
World countries will continue to suffer 7) _____ disasters, while the
rich countries consume the vast majority of the world's 8) _____.
Animals are also at risk. It is feared that some 9) _____ may soon
10) _____ , as their natural 11) _____ are destroyed. In some
cases, the only way to save a rare species from extinction is to breed it
12) _____ .

B In the same way as above, use these words to complete the passage.

damage	bottle banks	conservation	campaign
public transport	exhaust fumes	recycle ' fuel
energy sources	greenhouse effect	wildlife	packaging

Here are some suggestions for practical 1) _____. Use less
2) _____ at home and at work. Persuade governments to pay for
research into alternative 3) _____ like solar power. 4) _____
paper, glass, metal, plastic and batteries as much as possible. Ask for
5) _____ for glass recycling at local supermarkets. Walk, cycle or use
6) _____ if possible, to cut down on car 7) _____, which
contribute to the 8) _____. 9) _____ for public transport systems
to be improved. Join one of the many pressure groups which work to
protect 10) _____ and the countryside.

C Answer these questions as fully as you can, in conversation or in writing.

1 How would you start an environmental campaign in your area?
2 How can we reduce the level of chemicals we are exposed to in our daily life – in food, in water and in the air?
3 What alternative energy sources do you think should be more fully researched?
4 Can we as individuals do more to protect our environment?
5 What do you think is the single greatest danger to the environment?

Crime and Punishment

A Complete the passage with some of these words. Do not use any word more than once.

judge	verdict	prisoner	jury	fined	prison	sentenced
guilty	innocent	witnesses	evidence	trial	court	

The newspapers were full of reports of the murder 1) _____, which had lasted three weeks. The court had heard all the 2) _____ given by the four 3) _____. Now, at last, after staying out for several hours, the twelve men and women of the 4) _____ came back into 5) _____ and sat down. Tension was high in the public gallery and the 6) _____ looked very pale. The 7) _____ asked the jury for their 8) _____. After a moment's silence their reply was 9) '_____!' The judge therefore 10) _____ the man to fifteen years in 11) _____.

B Use these names of criminals to complete the definitions.

pickpocket	hijacker	blackmailer	burglar	shoplifter
	arsonist	kidnapper		

1 A(n) _____ takes over a plane or vehicle and forces the pilot or driver to go where he/she wants.

2 A(n) _____ takes away another person by force, usually to demand money.

3 A(n) _____ steals from people's pockets or bags, often in crowds.

4 A(n) _____ sets fire to buildings or cars on purpose.

5 A(n) _____ steals from a shop while pretending to be a customer.

6 A(n) _____ steals from a house or office, usually by breaking in.

C Choose the correct word from the pair in brackets to complete the sentences.

1 The lawyer who helps you to buy or sell your house, or to make a will, is a _____ . (barrister/solicitor)

2 If you are suspected of _____ a crime, you will probably be arrested. (committing/doing)

3 If the police arrest you, they must _____ you with a crime. (charge/accuse)

4 A person who breaks into your house, usually at night, to steal valuables is a _____. (robber/burglar)

5 If something is stolen from your flat, you should report the _____ to your insurance company. (thief/theft)

D Answer these questions as fully as you can, in conversation or in writing.

1 Do you think there is more crime now than there used to be?

2 What reasons do people have for committing crimes?

3 Is capital punishment suitable for certain crimes? If so, which ones?

4 How can crime be prevented or controlled?

5 Is prison a good punishment for criminals?

Health and Fitness

A Complete the passage with some of these words. Do not use any word or phrase more than once.

homeopathy	infectious	alternative medicine	conditions
medical	cure	treatment	incurable	operation
acupuncture	symptoms	immunized	injection

In most countries, children can now be 1) _____ against 2)_____ diseases such as polio and TB. Doctors can also offer 3)_____ for some of the diseases once considered 4)_____, like certain types of cancer. However, there are other serious 5)_____, such as AIDS, for which there is still no 6)_____, in spite of the millions of pounds being spent on 7)_____ research. One criticism of traditional medicine is that it treats only the 8)_____ of illness, not the causes. This has led to a growing interest in all areas of 9)_____, such as 10)_____, which offers a system for treating the whole person. 11)_____ and aromatherapy are also growing in popularity.

B In the same way as above, use these words to complete the passage.

stress	exercise	go on a diet	jogging	addicted
overweight	giving up	crash diets	relaxation
keep fit	weight	aerobics

People are much more interested in their health these days. Many people try to 1) _____ by taking 2) _____ two or three times a week, perhaps by going for a swim, by 3) _____ in the local park, or by playing active games like squash or tennis. 4) _____ classes are also popular. Most doctors recommend 5) _____ smoking as a good way of improving fitness. Being 6) _____ can be harmful to health, so many people decide to 7) _____ to try to lose 8) _____. Another problem for our health is the 9 _____ which affects many of us in our daily life. Fortunately there are simple 10) _____ techniques which can be learned to help deal with this. A relaxed life-style, a balanced diet and plenty of fresh air and exercise – these things are all important.

C Answer these questions as fully as you can, in conversation or in writing.

1 Work out a plan for keeping fit and healthy, considering
  a) exercise   b) diet   c) life-style.
2 Should smoking be banned in public places?
3 A doctor helped a patient to die by giving him a fatal injection. The patient was suffering from an incurable disease, was in great pain, and had asked to die. Was the doctor right or wrong?
4 How can governments help people to improve their health?
5 Imagine the advantages and disadvantages of a doctor's or nurse's job.

UNIT 48

Travel and Holidays

A Complete the passage with some of these words. Do not use any word or phrase more than once.

check in	bed and breakfast	package holiday
accommodation	resort	charter flight	scheduled flight
self-catering	insurance	cruise	brochures	passengers

A 1) _____ is one where the flight and 2) _____ are included in the price. These holidays are advertised in travel companies' 3) _____. You can choose which country and which 4) _____ to visit, and decide whether you want full or half board, or perhaps just 5) _____. But if you prefer to organize your holiday yourself, you can simply rent a 6) _____ apartment and make your own travel arrangements. If you are travelling on a 7) _____, remember that all 8) _____ should 9) _____ very early at the airport. And, whatever type of holiday you choose, it is a good idea to take out travel 10) _____, in case anything goes wrong.

B Match the people and type of holiday with the most suitable type of accommodation. Use each type of accommodation only once.

hotel	chalet	tent	bungalow	villa	apartment	youth hostel

1 two boys – camping   _____
2 large family needing a lot of space – beach   _____
3 family wanting to save money – self-catering   _____
4 group of friends – skiing   _____
5 businessman and wife – city   _____
6 two students – walking   _____

C Choose the correct word from the pair in brackets to complete the sentences.

1 We went on a marvellous round-the-world _____. (travel/trip)
2 Jim has booked a three-week _____ round the Greek islands. (cruise/voyage)
3 It takes Helen half an hour to _____ from home to school. (journey/travel)
4 The holiday included a one-day _____ to Ephesus. (excursion/sightseeing)
5 We decided to go on a _____ of European capitals. (drive/tour)

D Answer these questions as fully as you can, in conversation or in writing.

1 What are the advantages and disadvantages of travelling alone?
2 Do you prefer a relaxing holiday or an activity holiday?
3 Do you prefer to plan a holiday in advance, or to make a last-minute decision to go somewhere?
4 How much holiday do you think people need every year?
5 What is your ideal holiday?

Science and Technology

A Complete the passage with some of these words. Do not use any word more than once.

scientists	laboratories	mass production
microchip	experiments	invention research
labour-saving	progress	automatic factories
vending machines	technology	

Experts claim that progress is being made in all scientific fields, and in many cases they are right. In 1) _____ all round the world, 2) _____ carry out many 3) _____ and do important 4) _____ into ways of improving technology. Machinery has already replaced large numbers of workers in many 5) _____, and prices of electrical goods have been reduced by 6) _____. Many of us are now quite used to the convenience of getting stamps, snacks and soft drinks from 7) _____, and we are able to use 8) _____ domestic appliances to make housework easier. Perhaps the 9) _____ which has made the most dramatic difference to life in developed countries is the 10) _____ in our computers. However, we cannot call this 11) _____ if our quality of life suffers as 12) _____ becomes more complicated.

B Match each activity with a type of equipment. Write the correct letter next to the number on the right.

1	wash clothes	A	freezer	1 ___
2	heat up food	B	vacuum cleaner	2 ___
3	listen to music	C	air conditioning	3 ___
4	wash plates and glasses	D	fax machine	4 ___
5	clean the carpet	E	video recorder	5 ___
6	write a letter	F	word processor	6 ___
7	store food for months	G	microwave (oven)	7 ___
8	prepare food	H	dishwasher	8 ___
9	keep rooms cool	I	washing machine	9 ___
10	send an instant letter	J	calculator	10 ___
11	do quick arithmetic	K	CD player	11 ___
12	watch a programme televised yesterday	L	food processor	12 ___

C Answer these questions as fully as you can, in conversation or in writing.

1 What are some of the advantages and disadvantages of modern technology?

2 Does everybody need to know how to use a computer these days?

3 Is life safer, or more dangerous, with modern technology?

4 If you were on a desert island, what piece of modern equipment would you miss the most? Why?

5 Which area of future scientific research do you think is most important?

Food and Drink

A Complete the passage with some of these words. Do not use any word or phrase more than once.

vegetarian	eat out	cook	vegan	cookery books
take-away	recipes	fast food	snack	ingredients
starter	main course	restaurants	dessert	
	menu	protein	meal	

If you're a 1) _____, you avoid eating meat and sometimes fish. If you're a 2) _____, you try not to eat any animal products at all. Although many 3) _____ now offer vegetarian menus, cooking your own food is the easiest way of eating what you like. A three-course meal begins with the 4) _____, then the 5) _____ follows, and finally there is the 6) _____, but you may decide to serve just one really interesting dish. Most 7) _____ in 8) _____ are not difficult to use, if you make sure you have all the right 9) _____. When it's ready, you can serve the 10) _____ to your family and friends. But if you're tired or too busy to 11) _____, you may decide you'd rather 12) _____, or get a 13) _____ to eat at home.

B Write one type of food next to the way it is often cooked. Think carefully because you must use each type of food only once.

cream	rice	eggs	beef	ice-cream	chips	bread	steak

1 boil _____   5 fry _____

2 scramble _____   6 grill _____

3 roast _____   7 whip _____

4 bake _____   8 freeze _____

C In each group, one type of food or drink is the odd one out. Circle the word which is different from the others in its group.

1 strawberry apple onion melon
2 carrot potato cabbage orange
3 beef mutton sheep veal
4 fig aubergine courgette cucumber
5 milk lemon cheese butter cream
6 bread biscuit pasta cake jam
7 salt flour pepper chilli mustard
8 egg tomato lamb fish chicken
9 tea lemonade coffee chocolate
10 wine beer cider milk

D Answer these questions as fully as you can, in conversation or in writing.

1 Why do you think people become vegetarians?
2 Can you describe your favourite recipe?
3 What is a balanced diet?
4 What foods and drinks are good or bad for your health?
5 What daily timetable would you recommend for meals?

People and Lifestyles

A Complete the passage with some of these words. Do not use any word or phrase more than once.

superstars	flying visit	hospitably	privacy	popular
ambition	afford	autographs	well-off	
publicity	respect	standard of living		

It's a real thrill to meet 1) _____ in the flesh. And that's exactly what happened to the people of Lower Norton, when the Rolling Stones paid a(n) 2) _____ to the village. 'It's always been my 3) _____ ,' Stephanie Heath, aged 15, told us, 'to meet a real live pop star! And now I've met five!' The Stones were travelling by private plane to Bristol, when bad weather forced the pilot to make an emergency landing in a field close to Lower Norton. They were 4) _____ entertained by the villagers, who took the opportunity of asking for 5) _____ . However, despite the excitement of the event, people were careful to 6) _____ the stars' desire for 7) _____ , and rooms were made available for them at the local pub. The story has given the Stones some useful 8) _____ in the area, and they are currently the most 9) _____ group among the teenagers of Lower Norton.

B Choose the correct word from the pair in brackets to complete the sentences.

1 Douglas didn't mind living _____ at all. In fact, he quite enjoyed it. (lonely/alone)

2 Jessica won the Newburg scholarship, which gave her the _____ of studying in Boston. (possibility/opportunity)

3 Our new neighbours must be fairly _____ : they're having a swimming pool built. (wealthy/luxury)

4 The headmaster sighed. He was counting the days to his _____ . (retirement/retreat)

5 The Jeffersons have a charming _____ in the Lake District where they spend their holidays. (summer-house/second home)

6 Malik's parents have a large _____ house, with a beautiful garden all round it. (detached/one-family)

7 Andy and his friends live like _____ on an old houseboat on the Thames. They haven't got jobs, but can just about get by on social security payments. (yuppies/hippies)

C Answer these questions as fully as you can, in conversation or in writing.

1 Which famous person would you like to meet, and why?

2 Would you like to be famous? What problems are there for famous people?

3 Do you think your lifestyle will be different from your parents', or the same? Describe the way you think you will live in the future.

4 What things can make people change their lifestyle? Can you think of examples of people whose way of life has changed dramatically?

5 What is the single most important thing in your life, and why?

UNIT 52

Relationships

A Complete the passage with some of these words. Do not use any word or phrase more than once.

fiancée	engagement	get married	engaged	wedding
marriage	reception	honeymoon	fell in love	go out with
bride	bridegroom	best man	bridesmaids	divorced

On the day Paul met Catherine, he asked her to 1) _____ him. They began to spend a lot of time together, and gradually they 2) _____. Six months after they met, they decided to 3) _____. Paul's family were very pleased when he introduced his 4) _____ to them, and Catherine's parents were delighted that their daughter was 5) _____ to such a nice young man. The wedding 6) _____ was going to be held in a hotel and the young couple planned to spend their 7) _____ on a romantic island in the Caribbean. On the day of the 8) _____ the church was full. The 9) _____ was waiting there, with his eldest brother, who was his 10) _____ . Why was Catherine so late? At home on the other side of town, the 11) _____ was also waiting, with her 12) _____, for the wedding cars to arrive. Her father had booked them for the wrong time. Fortunately the ceremony took place in the end!

B In the same way as above, use these words to complete the passage.

teenager	respected	argued	jealous
generation gap	fond of	broke off	drifted apart
relationship	only child	friendship	

At the age of 16, Maurice went to work in his uncle Stephen's shop. His uncle was an elderly man who had nothing in common with a 1) _____ , but despite the 2) _____ Maurice got on well with him. Although they sometimes 3) _____, Maurice always 4) _____ his uncle's opinions. But one day, another employee who was 5) _____ of Maurice told Stephen that his nephew had stolen money from the shop. Maurice was shocked to discover that his uncle believed the story. Stephen 6) _____ his working 7) _____ with Maurice, who had to find another job. After that, they 8) _____, and only saw each other at family gatherings.

C Answer these questions as fully as possible, in conversation or in writing.

1 Should boys and girls be treated differently during their childhood?
2 What are the most common problems between parents and teenagers?
3 Should a mother stay at home to look after her children while they are young?
4 Should old people be cared for by their children or sent to old people's homes?
5 What are the advantages and disadvantages of being an only child?

Entertainment and the Media

A Complete the passage with some of these words. Do not use any word or phrase more than once.

screen	stage	panel	live	press
audience	broadcast	admission	tickets	
rehearsal	recorded	box office	presenter	applause

Radio shows are often 1) _____ in towns around the country, in front of a studio 2) _____ , and then 3) _____ to the public at a later date. Quiz shows and panel games are particularly popular, especially as in most cases 4) _____ is free. You just have to keep an eye out for advance warning in the local 5) _____ , and then send off for your 6) _____ . Recording will probably take place in a theatre or concert hall, with the celebrities sitting round a table on the 7) _____ , and a chairman or 8) _____ in charge of the proceedings. There may be a brief sound check, or even a short 9) _____ , if participants need to practise what they're going to say, and then the fun starts. Even the 10) _____ is faithfully recorded, so if you listen to the programme on the radio later, you may hear yourself clapping enthusiastically!

B Choose the correct word from the pair in brackets to complete the sentences.

1 Yes, I had a wonderful weekend. It was great _____ . (fun/funny)
2 Good afternoon, _____ , and welcome to another series of your favourite quiz show, Count Down! (viewers/spectators)
3 Have you read the _____ of your friend's play in the local paper? (critic/review)
4 If you buy a _____ , you can attend all the concerts at a reduced price. (discount ticket/season ticket)
5 Meryl Streep gave one of her best _____ in Out of Africa. (roles/performances)
6 They'll never forget seeing the Beatles _____ in concert. (live/alive)
7 Our next celebrity _____ needs no introduction. Ladies and gentlemen, please welcome Frank Bruno. (host/guest)
8 Most people agree that Fellini was a truly _____ film director. (great/big)
9 I'll _____ you tonight at 8 o'clock. Then we'll just be in time for the start of the film. (call for/call at)

C Answer these questions as fully as you can, in conversation or in writing.

1 Suggest a suitable day's entertainment for the following people: (a) some elderly relatives (b) a business friend of your parents' (c) a teenage cousin (d) a young couple with a baby (e) your nephew aged 6.
2 Do you prefer listening to live or recorded music? Give your reasons.
3 Which do you think is better, reading a book or watching the film of the book? Why?
4 What would your ideal evening out involve?

Money and Shopping

A Complete the passage with some of these words. Do not use any word or phrase more than once.

budget	deposit account	interest	cheque book	pay in
current account	credit card	withdraw	overdraft
statement	purchases	account	cash

It's quite easy nowadays to open an 1) _____ at a bank. You fill in some forms and 2) _____ some money. You're usually given a 3) _____ to use when shopping, instead of carrying 4) _____. You can also ask for a 5) _____, which is useful in restaurants and hotels, and for making large 6) _____. Your first bank account is normally a 7) _____. You can pay in or 8) _____ money as often as you like, as long as you don't run up a large 9) _____! You will receive a regular 10) _____, which shows what has been paid in and withdrawn. But if you want to save money, a 11) _____ is better, because the bank pays you 12) _____ on your savings.

B In the same way as above, use these words to complete the sentences.

| exchange rate | note | coins | currency | mortgage | change |
| deposit | tax | income | cheque | wages | balance |

1 The one pound _____ has been abolished in England and replaced by a coin.

2 If you're going abroad, you'll need to take some foreign _____ with you.

3 Excuse me, I need some _____ for the phone. Have you got any 20p or 50p _____?

4 He's not going to transfer the money to his account abroad until the _____ goes up.

5 Their _____ payments are very high, but at least the house will be theirs in a few years' time.

6 If you put down a _____ on the television, sir, you can pay the rest in monthly instalments.

7 Every year we have to fill in a form for the _____ office, giving details of our _____.

8 Do you mind if I pay by _____? I seem to have run out of cash.

C Answer these questions as fully as possible, in conversation or in writing.

1 How do you manage your money? Do you have a budget?

2 What are the advantages and disadvantages of credit cards?

3 Do you ever lend or borrow money?

4 Would you like to have more money than your parents? What difference would being very rich make to you?

5 Do you think money should be saved or spent?

Formal Letters

Practise using these phrases.
Remember – do not use short forms.

Dear Sir or Madam, ... Yours faithfully,

Dear Mr Smith, ... Yours sincerely,

Thank you for your letter of 2nd May.

With reference to your letter of 2nd May, ...

I would like to say ......

I should point out that ......

I would like to inform you ......

I regret to inform you ......

I have pleasure in enclosing ......

I hope that will not inconvenience you.

Would you be kind enough to ....?

I would be grateful if you would ......

I was especially impressed by ......

I hope you will be able to offer some explanation for this.

Thank you in advance for your help.

I look forward to receiving your prompt reply.

Sample question and answer

You and a colleague, Liz, are arranging to stay in or near Oxford, so that you can attend a weekend conference. Read your colleague's note and your own notes, and write a letter of between 120 and 180 words in an appropriate style to the hotel manager. Do not include addresses.

Jane:

Confirm & send a cheque

I've booked the Charlecote Hotel by phone for Friday and Saturday 9 & 10 February, but they want a £20 deposit for each of us. I'm not sure if I asked for two singles or not. We'll probably have dinner both nights, but remember I'm vegetarian! And can you arrange transport to the conference?

Tell them!   *taxi?*   *Confirm*

Thanks, Liz

Dear Sir or Madam,

I would like to confirm the telephone booking made by my colleague Liz King for two nights, Friday and Saturday 9 and 10 February. We would like two single rooms, with en suite bathrooms if possible. **I have pleasure in enclosing** a cheque for £40, as a deposit for both of us.

We would like to have dinner in the hotel on both nights, but **I should point out that** Ms King is a vegetarian. **I hope that will not inconvenience you**.

As we will be attending the IBF Conference in Oxford on Saturday and Sunday, we would like you to book a taxi for us, to arrive at the Brandon Hall Conference Centre by 9 a.m. each day.

We will be arriving at about 5 p.m. on Friday, and are looking forward to our stay at the Charlecote.

Yours faithfully,

Jane Fernandez (Ms)

A Choose the words or expressions in the box which are appropriate for a formal letter and circle them.

> Sorry!   On the other hand,   Hello   However,
> Your friend,   In addition,   How's the wife?   Dear boss,
> Love and kisses,   Well,   a nice guy   Thanks a lot
> All the best,   approximately   Furthermore,   Therefore
> you see,   Have fun!   See you soon,   Yours faithfully,
> I apologize   I intend to   Don't worry,   It's nice of you

B Complete the following formal letter with the correct form of the verbs in brackets.

Dear Sir or Madam,

When I (arrive) in England last year, I (open) a current bank account at your branch. Now I (come) to the end of my language course, and (take) my final examination next week. In another fortnight I (go) back to Italy, so I (like) (close) my account. I (write) (ask) you (transfer) the balance to my account in Rome: I (already give) you the details of this.

Please (you send) me a statement (show) my balance and also details of transfer charges. I (return) my chequebook and credit card to you by 23rd January. That is the date I (like) the account (be closed).

Thank you for your attention. (I look forward to) (receive) your reply.

Yours faithfully,

Giovanni Zeffirelli

C Now write one or both of these compositions, using between 120 and 180 words. **Remember** –
- read the question carefully and plan your answer;
- cover all the points in the question;
- check your spelling, grammar and punctuation;
- do not use colloquial English or slang;
- do not include addresses;
- write the correct number of words.

1 You have just returned from a holiday which was not at all what you expected. You are writing a letter of complaint to the travel agent who arranged it for you. Read carefully the notes you made during the holiday. Then write your letter to the travel agent, covering the points in your notes and adding any relevant information about your travelling companions.

- no coach waiting for us at airport, brochure said this was included
- taxis in resort very expensive!
- hotel miles from the beach
- room rather small for three of us and dirty
- no clean towels during holiday, two whole weeks!
- resort was crowded and noisy, described as 'quiet' by travel agent

2 You are interested in a job you have seen advertised. Look at the advertisement and write a letter of application for the post.

> SECRETARY/RECEPTIONIST NEEDED
> Have you got a good telephone manner?
> Have you got VDU/PC skills?
> Can you work under pressure?
> If so, contact the Personnel Manager,
> Seeboard, 12 Church Road, Hove, BN3 2TG.

Informal Letters

Practise using these phrases. **Remember** – use short forms and conversational English.

Dear (name) ......

Yours,/Regards,/Best wishes,/Love (from)

It seems ages since I last wrote.

I've been meaning to write to you for ages.

What's your new flat/job/boss like?

It would be really nice to see you again.

I do hope you can come.　Anyway ......　　By the way, ...

Do let me know as soon as possible.

All the best to your parents / Give my regards to your parents.

Looking forward to hearing from you soon.

Sample question and answer

You have not written to or seen a friend for some time. Write to him or her to explain why, and also to invite him/her to a party you are giving soon.

Dear Tim,

It seems ages since I last wrote. How are you these days? **What's your new flat like**? I'm looking forward to seeing it. Perhaps I could come up for a weekend sometime and help you paint a couple of rooms.

I know I should have written before, and **I've been meaning to write to you for ages**, but I've had to do lots of overtime at the office. My new boss is awful! But no doubt I'll get used to him soon.

Anyway, to cheer myself up, I've decided to have a party. **I do hope you can come**. It'll be in two weeks' time, on Saturday 15th February, at my place. It'll start at about 8.30 p.m. There'll be a bit of food, but not much. I can offer you a bed for the night, on the sofa!

It would be really nice to see you again. Looking forward to hearing from you soon.

Best wishes,

Mark

A Turn these formal sentences into more informal language. To help you, the final word is given.

1 I apologize for my unpunctuality.

_____ late.

2 Our accommodation must be arranged.

_____ stay.

3 Please accept my thanks for your help.

_____ help.

4 I would like to enquire whether you have reached a decision.

_____ yet?

5 There is very little likelihood of your achieving a pass.

_____ fail.

6 I look forward to receiving your prompt reply.

_____ soon.

7 You have committed a serious error.

_____ mistake.

B Complete the informal letter using the expressions from the box.

let me know	By the way	What's the new office like
Any chance	Never mind	Remember If you like
What do you think	Congratulations	or something

Dear Silvia,

It was lovely to get your letter. How awful about your holiday! They really should have told you the hotel wouldn't be near the beach. 1) _____ , it'll be different when you and I go next summer. You won't be disappointed, I promise! 2) _____ , it's my sister's villa we're going to, so I've been before and know the area really well. 3) _____ , she says there's a new swimming pool nearby, so bring your swimsuit!

4) _____ on getting your promotion at last! 5) _____ ? I hope you've got your name on the door!

6) _____ of seeing you one weekend? 7) _____ , we could meet in London for a meal and go to an exhibition 8) _____ .

9) _____ ? Give me a ring and 10) _____ .

    Love,
    Pam

C Now write one or more of these compositions, using between 120 and 180 words. **Remember –**
- read the question carefully and plan your answer;
- cover all the points in the question;
- check your spelling, grammar and punctuation;
- use short forms and colloquial English;
- do not include addresses;
- write the correct number of words.

1 You are organizing a school trip to France, and have decided you need an extra helper, so you are going to ask your friend, Joe, to join you. Read the notes below and write him an informal letter.

    Dates: 22 July to 5 August (2 weeks)
    Number of children: 21. Ages: 10-12.
    Helpers: 1 teacher, 2 parents, one more needed (Joe?)
    Accommodation : boarding school near Bordeaux.
    Transport: coach. Activities: walking/windsurfing, sailing.
    Cost: free to teachers or helpers!

2 This is part of a letter you receive from your aunt, mentioning her daughter, your cousin. Write a letter to Joanna, giving as much helpful advice as you can.

    You probably know that Joanna is just about to start studying at university. Have you got any tips for her? Things to remember, things to avoid? I'd be very grateful if you could write to her.

3 You have received the following invitation from an old friend you have not seen for a long time. Unfortunately, you will be unable to go to the party. Write to him explaining why you have to refuse the invitation, and giving information about yourself and other friends you have seen recently.

    You are invited to a New Year's Eve Party
    at 8.30 p.m. on Saturday 31st December
    at 25 Beverley Close, Cambridge, CB2 7CH.
    RSVP to Roy Bailey at the above address.

Articles and Reports

> **An article** is a piece of writing for a newspaper or magazine. It can be interesting and entertaining as well as informative. There is often a title or heading, which may be a word, a short phrase, a sentence or a question. Remember that the style or register used depends on the topic and on the kind of people who will be reading the newspaper or magazine.

Sample question and answer

An international student magazine is printing a series of articles on 'Living Abroad'. Write a short article for the magazine on this topic, based on your own experience if possible.

Living Abroad

The first thing you should realize is that it might take you a while to get used to living in another country, because you will probably miss your family and friends a lot in the first few weeks. All sorts of things may be different – the food, the daily timetable, the customs, the weather and the language. The last of these is, in a way, the most important, as you need to be able to communicate in order to make the most of your stay. So I advise you to find a good school, where you'll make new friends and improve your language skills.

When you can socialize and talk to people, you'll feel more confident, and will really start to enjoy yourself. That's a good time to explore all the entertainment and sporting facilities in the school, town or village where you're staying, or even travel round the country. If you maintain a positive attitude, you will certainly have a good time, and take lots of memorable experiences back home with you.

A Invent a short title for each article on the following subjects.

1 Learning a language in the country where it is spoken may be more expensive, but it usually produces results much more rapidly.

_____

2 Pollution is now a major world problem, and all countries should work together on ways of reducing it. More research should be done into sources of alternative energy.

_____

3 Animals are excellent companions for elderly people whose children have grown up and left home or who live alone for any reason.

_____

4 Cars should be banned from town centres, to protect pedestrians, reduce exhaust fumes and improve traffic flow. More people would use public transport if it were cheaper and more efficient.

_____

5 T-shirts and jeans are just another kind of uniform, worn by thousands of people around the world. People who are slaves to fashion have lost their individuality.

_____

> **A report** is a factual description of events or situations and may include suggestions for future action. It should be written in a formal style, with a clear layout. Titles or headings, if used, should be short and simple. Remember to refer specifically to the task when writing a report.

Sample question and answer

You have recently started work for a large company, who sent you on a two-week language course to improve your English. Now you have to write a report for your boss. Write your report, describing the school and the course, and commenting on both good and bad points.

English International is a large school in the south of England, well placed for day-trips to London. Because all classes are multi-national, students have to use English almost all the time, which is excellent. The buildings are attractive and the classrooms spacious. Teachers are both qualified and experienced, and I found them very helpful.

The school specializes in teaching Business English to advanced students, so it was a good choice for me. Their facilities are good. Teachers use video and computers in the classroom, and students can use the supervised self-access area after school. There is no charge for this, so we could study all day if we wished, at no extra cost.

The course was well organized, with 25 lessons a week, covering all four language skills. Unfortunately, there were one or two weaker students in my class, so the pace was rather slow for me. I would also have liked more writing practice.

On the whole, however, I would recommend a course at this school. The atmosphere was excellent, and the lessons were stimulating. I certainly feel I made considerable progress.

B Choose the words or expressions in the box which are appropriate for a report, and circle them.

a smashing place	excellent facilities	What a pity!
Moreover,	I haven't a clue	I would like to recommend ...
How about going ...?	I had a great time	Thanks for sending me
The teachers were great	Guess what?	In general, Why bother?
Another disadvantage ...	Have a good trip!	In conclusion,
I can't wait to go again	You'd love it!	superb accommodation

C Now write one or more of these compositions, using between 120 and 180 words. **Remember –**
- read the question carefully and plan your answer;
- cover all the points in the question;
- check your spelling, grammar and punctuation;
- use an appropriate style and the correct number of words.

1 Write an article for a competition in a young people's magazine on
  a) modern music   or
  b) advice to tourists visiting your country   or
  c) how to learn a language.

2 Write an article on a new film or play which you have seen recently, for a students' art magazine.

3 Write a report for your fellow-students on the types of entertainment available in your town.

4 Write a report for your teacher on:
  a) a book you have recently read or studied   or
  b) an excursion you have recently been on.

Narrative Compositions and Set Texts

Narrative compositions
Practise using these words and phrases. **Remember** – use the Past Continuous to set the scene, the Past Perfect for flashbacks and previous actions or preparations, and the Past Simple for actions. Make a plan, and use paragraphs.

As soon as ......   I was just about to ...... when ......

Although ......   Despite ......   Sometimes ....

Suddenly ......   Just then ......

When we reached the top / house / town, I saw ......

I was surprised / delighted / horrified to find ......

To my surprise / horror / amazement I saw that ......

It wasn't until ...... that I noticed / realized ......

No sooner had I ...... than ......

Suddenly I realized I had left my passport / money / sandwiches at home.

Eventually ......   At last ......   Just as ......

It was the best / worst day / holiday I had ever had.

Luckily, nobody was badly hurt / injured.

It had been a very enjoyable / exciting / tiring day.

It was a great relief to ......

It had been quite an adventure.

Sample question and answer
You and your friends went on a walk to explore your local countryside recently. Describe what happened.

It was a beautiful morning when we set off. The air was still cool, and the birds were singing. Bob had persuaded us to have a country walk and picnic, starting from his village, and I was proudly wearing my new walking boots.

As soon as we had left the village we found the footpath. The sun began to get hotter as we walked across the fields. **Sometimes** we stopped to look at wild flowers, and Bob knew most of their names.

After a few hours we reached a lake, and stopped to eat our sandwiches. **It wasn't until** I sat down **that I realized** how much my feet hurt. I lay down for a rest, but **no sooner had I** closed my eyes **than** Bob jumped up, saying we should set off again.

The footpath seemed much longer on the way back, and my feet hurt so much that I could hardly walk. **At last** the village came into view. **It was a great relief to** get back to Bob's house, and take my boots off!

A Look at the following sentences, which come at the beginning of a story. Write one suitable sentence to follow each one.

1 Bettina opened the door and screamed.

_____

2 Jonathan picked up the book and noticed its title.

_____

3 The letter dropped on to the doormat, and Zora picked it up.

_____

4 When Rupert went into the manager's office, he had a feeling he knew what would happen.

_____

Now look at the following sentences, which come at the end of a story. Write a suitable sentence **before** each one.

5 _____

Fortunately, however, we reached our destination safely.

6 _____

The chairman signed the paper and handed it to me with a smile.

7 _____

They bundled the man into their car and took him away.

8 _____

She sighed happily and lay back in her chair.

B Now write one or more of these compositions, using between 120 and 180 words. **Remember** –
• check your grammar, spelling and punctuation;
• write the correct number of words.

1 You were walking down a street when you saw an accident. Describe what you saw and what you did next.
2 You and an old schoolfriend met by chance in the street and decided to spend the rest of the day together. Describe what you did.
3 You went on a day's excursion to a big town with several friends. Describe the day's activities.
4 Describe the best or worst holiday you've ever had.
5 Write a story ending with the words *I was very relieved to get home safe and sound.*

When writing about **set texts**, it is important to read the question carefully and plan your answer, using paragraphs with linking words. Refer to the story to support your opinions, and to show that you are familiar with the book. Make the composition as interesting as possible, by using a wide range of vocabulary and structures. Above all, give enough details so that someone who had not read the book would be able to understand your account.

C Use the following linking words or phrases to join the two halves of the sentences: *because, although, where, (so) ... that, but, in order to.*

1 Adela Quested went to India
2 Eliza learns to speak like a lady
3 Ronald planned the murder so well
4 Owen hated his brother
5 Olivia killed her husband
6 Maurice was going to Australia

A _____ marry Stephen Castle.
B _____ decided not to live there.
C _____ he was jealous of him.
D _____ she's only a Cockney flower girl.
E _____ his fiancée lived.
F _____ he was sure he'd never be found out.

D Now write one or more of these compositions, based on your reading of a particular set book. Use between 120 and 180 words. **Remember** –
• include details from the book.

1 Can you explain why the author used this title for the book?
2 Who do you like or dislike most in the book? Explain why.
3 Do you think the story should have had a different ending? Explain your ideas.
4 Write a letter to a character in the book, commenting on his/her behaviour and explaining how you would have acted differently.
5 Write a report on the book for a group of students who have not read it. Say whether you would recommend it or not.

Discursive Compositions

Practise using these words and phrases. **Remember** – make a plan and use paragraphs. Do not use short forms.

> The main advantage of ...... is ......   One advantage of ...... is ......
>
> A point in favour of ... is ......   Besides ......   As well as ...
>
> Another point is that ......   Another advantage is ......   Moreover ......
>
> Another problem is ......   In contrast ......
>
> The biggest disadvantage is ......   On one hand, ...
>
> On the other hand, ...   However, ...   Nevertheless, ...
>
> Whereas ......   While ......   In spite of ......   Despite ......
>
> It is worth remembering that ......   On balance, ...
>
> In conclusion, ...   To sum up, ...   On the whole, ...

Sample question, plan and answer

Would you prefer to live in a town or in the country? Give your reasons.

Town	Country
+ more convenient for shopping, studying, work, entertainment	+ quieter, more relaxing life
+ better public transport, so cheaper	+ better, cleaner air, so healthier
– polluted air	+ more space for everybody
– noise (traffic, neighbours)	– long way from work, shops, schools, nightlife
– less space	– expensive transport

The main advantage of living in town is that it is much more convenient for studying, working and shopping. Towns offer better facilities for entertainment **as well as** better job opportunities. **Besides**, public transport is usually more efficient in a town, which makes travelling to school or work cheaper and easier.

On the other hand, certain aspects of living in a town can be unpleasant. There is often a lot of noise from traffic or even from neighbours, **whereas** life in the country is considerably more peaceful. **Moreover**, the air in towns is often seriously polluted by exhaust fumes, **while** country air is cleaner and healthier.

Another point in favour of living in the country is that there is more open space for children and adults to enjoy. There is also the opportunity to observe wildlife more closely.

On balance, I would say that **despite** the advantages of living in a town, I would prefer to lead a quieter, more relaxing life in the country.

A Make a plan for these composition topics, similar to the sample plan. Use the words in brackets if possible.

1   Do you prefer travelling by plane or by train?
    (comfortable/expensive/convenient)

2   What kind of pet is most suitable for a family with two young children living in the suburbs?
    (space/exercise/walk the dog/companionship/be responsible for)

3   Should you live at home until you are married?
    (independence/freedom/rely on your family/generation gap/emotional support)

B Match the formal expressions on the left with the more informal ones of similar meaning. (Several answers may be possible.)

1 furthermore
2 in addition
3 therefore
4 however
5 for this reason
6 moreover

A also
B so
C but
D as well
E and

C Use one of these linking words or phrases to join each pair of clauses or phrases: *where, while, although, despite, in case, as well as, so ... that*. Use each word or phrase once only.

1 Some towns have an underground railway system / others operate trams or trolleybuses.

2 People are often nervous of using computers / in fact you can learn the basic skills quite quickly.

3 Scientists have gone far in their research into space technology / they envisage setting up a scientific base in space very soon.

4 Hospital staff are still committed to the welfare of their patients / the fact that they feel undervalued by the health authority managers.

5 Making improvements in education involves considerable investment / the energy and enthusiasm of all concerned.

6 A lifeboat crew is always on call / a windsurfer gets into trouble or a boat capsizes.

7 New businesses are often set up in offices or shops / a previous business has just closed down.

D Complete the text with these linking words and phrases: *furthermore, on the other hand, to sum up, despite, to start with, in addition, whereas.*

A package holiday has several advantages over an independently organized one. 1) _____ , it is usually cheaper. 2) _____ , everything is included, so that the customer doesn't have to arrange anything.

3) _____ , there is normally a courier or representative at the resort who can sort out any problems that may arise.

4) _____ , you may not want to travel in a large group, or stay in an international-style hotel. So, 5) _____ the attractions of the package holiday, you may choose to make your own arrangements, for greater flexibility.

6) _____ , if you want an economical, lively holiday, a package is a good idea, 7) _____ if your aims are more ambitious you should organize your holiday yourself.

E Now write one or more of these compositions, using between 120 and 180 words. **Remember** –
• read the question carefully and plan your answer;
• cover all the points in the question;
• use formal English, and formal linking words.

Your school offers a prize for the best composition each year. These are the topics you can choose from:

1 'The best way to learn a language is to study it in the country where it is spoken.' Do you agree?

2 Which do you prefer as entertainment, watching a video at home or going out to the cinema? Give your reasons.

3 'Wild animals should not be kept in circuses, zoos or safari parks.' Do you agree?

4 How can people maintain good health and fitness these days?

5 What can be done about the international problem of pollution?

Descriptive Compositions

Describing people
Practise using these words and phrases. **Remember** – make a plan and use paragraphs.

straight / curly / wavy / greying / blond hair
a fringe   a parting   bald
bushy eyebrows   moustache   bearded
a hooked nose   a turned-up nose
gnarled hands   a weatherbeaten face
ears that stick out   red cheeks
tanned   freckled   wrinkled
a pale complexion   dimples   dark-skinned
a warm smile   a generous mouth
He looks young for his age.
She's in her early twenties / mid-thirties / late forties.
He's 1.70 metres tall.
smartly dressed   shabby   neat
He / she usually wears glasses / a jacket / jeans.
He is wearing a uniform / a peaked cap / his best suit / a three-piece suit / slippers / sandals / boots / trainers.
She is wearing an apron / a T-shirt / shorts / a summer dress.
You are immediately struck by ......
cheerful   easy to get on with   likeable   attractive
moody   bad-tempered   unpredictable   unreliable
Although ......   In fact, ...

Sample question and answer
Describe a member of your family, explaining the effect he or she has had on your life.

My uncle is quite a small man, and has a very **weatherbeaten** face, because he does a lot of sailing, even in winter. **Although** he is in his mid-fifties, with **greying hair** and a **bald** patch on top of his head, when you meet him **you are immediately struck by** his charm. He always greets you with **a warm smile**, and shows great interest in what you say.

Uncle Fred is a very important member of the family. Because my father died when I was very young, Uncle Fred helped my mother to bring me and my sisters up. He and his wife live near us, and they are constantly popping in or ringing up. I have always thought of him as a father, and I often go to him for advice.

In fact, I owe my future career to him, because he was the one who first encouraged me to study law. He will be delighted when I qualify as a lawyer next year.

Describing places and events
Practise using these words and phrases. **Remember** – make a plan and use paragraphs.

> When you enter the building, ...
>
> From there you see ......
>
> The first thing you notice is ......
>
> At first sight ......   Then you notice ......
>
> We tend to ......
>
> Sometimes people ......
>
> I am particularly impressed by ......
>
> I especially / particularly like ......
>
> My favourite place, though, is ......
>
> The impression you get is that ......
>
> It looks / looked as if ......
>
> On the anniversary of ......
>
> This is a very special occasion in my country because ......
>
> We always celebrate this day because ......
>
> There is always a wonderful atmosphere.
>
> People dance in the streets and let off fireworks.

Sample question and answer
Describe your dream home.

To get to my dream house, you have to drive up a long, winding lane for several miles, until you come to the big white gates. **From there you** get a good view of the house. It's a solid, square, Georgian house, with a gravel drive, a large lawn, and several ancient oak trees in front of the house.

It's right in the country, of course, a long way from any industry or pollution. **However,** there is a convenient railway station only a mile away.

The rooms are large and well furnished with antiques. **I especially like** the library, with its shelves of dusty leather-bound books. **My favourite place, though,** is the big walled garden, where the sun always seems to shine, and where I grow roses, vegetables and herbs.

Sometimes I spend hours imagining myself and my friends in this beautiful home. It seems very real to me.

Now write one or more of these compositions, using between 120 and 180 words. **Remember** –
- read the question carefully and plan your answer;
- cover all the points in the question;
- check your spelling, grammar and punctuation;
- make your description as interesting as possible.

Your teacher has asked you to write a description of the following:

1 A visit to a museum or art gallery which particularly interested you.
2 Your favourite shop, and why it appeals to you.
3 A person you have known for a long time, and why you like or dislike him or her.
4 A religious, national or local festival in your country.
5 The centre of your town or village, and the sort of people who can usually be seen there.

TEST 1

A Choose the correct word or phrase to complete each sentence. Write the letter in the space.

1 I am very interested _____ the courses you are organizing.

 a) on   b) in   c) to   d) for

2 I'm afraid I haven't got _____ change – only a £10 note.

 a) any   b) a lot   c) some   d) a

3 They work in offices _____ are air-conditioned.

 a) who   b) they   c) which   d) where

4 I'm going to _____ my suit dry-cleaned.

 a) make   b) have   c) take   d) let

5 If you don't start watching until 8.30 tonight, the programme _____ .

 a) will already have begun   b) will begin   c) has already begun
 d) had already begun

6 You can do your own cooking in a _____ apartment.

 a) camping   b) package   c) chalet   d) self-catering

7 It's sad that he has _____ friends of his own age.

 a) a little   b) little   c) few   d) a few

8 This is the best song _____ so far.

 a) I heard   b) I've heard   c) I hear   d) I'm hearing

9 They decided to have a picnic _____ the pouring rain.

 a) despite   b) on account   c) because   d) although

10 He didn't want to risk _____ late for the interview.

 a) arrive   b) arriving   c) to arrive   d) having arrived

11 I'd love to try and make that cake. Have you got a(n) _____ for it?

 a) receipt   b) prescription   c) ingredient   d) recipe

12 His car's in the car park, so he _____ be here.

 a) can   b) ought   c) must   d) needs to

13 You'd better see a doctor, _____ you?

 a) hadn't   b) didn't   c) wouldn't   d) don't

14 I wish I _____ my letter of application earlier.

 a) would write   b) had written   c) have written   d) wrote

15 That's the _____ difficult textbook I've ever used.

 a) more   b) even   c) most   d) very

16 Because Denise's parents worked abroad, they sent her to a _____ school.

 a) college   b) secondary   c) training   d) boarding

17 The helicopter landed _____ the roof of the building.

 a) at   b) in   c) over   d) on

18 I have a monthly bank _____ sent to me, so that I know how much there is in my account.

 a) balance   b) overdraft   c) statement   d) cheque

19 Meat can be stored for several months in a home _____ .

 a) freezer   b) fridge   c) cool box   d) cooler

20 If Jamal _____ on holiday, he'll spend a lot of money.

 a) will go   b) goes   c) would go   d) went

B Complete the passage, using one word for each space.

At an international conference 1) _____ the Canary Islands experts 2) _____ been discussing 3) _____ man's age. The man's dead 4) _____ was found by chance in the Alps last year. He was 5) _____ a skier 6) _____ had died in a recent accident, but 7) _____ unknown man who died 8) _____ 5000 years 9) _____ . His body was 10) _____ , well preserved, in a glacier. He was a short man, only 1.60 metres 11) _____ , and dark–skinned. It is not 12) _____ which race he belonged to. 13) _____ he is reported to have 14) _____ strong and well-built, he died of hunger. 15) _____ must have been difficult to 16) _____ food in those days. No doubt the weapons found by his side 17) _____ occasionally used in self-defence against 18) _____ hungry men. The 19) _____ of this 'iceman' may well 20) _____ solved when scientists subject his body to the radiocarbon-dating process.

C Complete the second sentence so that it has a similar meaning to the first. Use between two and five words, including the word given. Do not change the word given.

1 The boy broke his arm when he fell.   FALLEN
   If the boy _____ not have broken his arm.
2 You ought to put away all those toys before supper.   SHOULD
   All those toys _____ before supper.
3 The carpenter made a table for Alicia.   HAD
   Alicia _____ the carpenter.
4 Because of the traffic jam, Andrew couldn't get to the interview on time.
   FROM
   The traffic jam _____ to the interview on time.
5 I'm sure it isn't necessary to show your passport.   YOU
   I'm sure _____ your passport.
6 I'll have to start my journey home now.   I
   It's _____ my journey home.
7 Henry's more intelligent than Patrick.   AS
   Patrick _____ Henry.
8 'Would you open the window, Nicola?' said the teacher.   ASKED
   The teacher _____ the window.

D Complete the sentences with the correct form of a phrasal verb with **look** or **take.**

1 When Frank moves to Geneva, he'll have to _____ a flat.
2 The doctor asked Antonio to _____ his shirt.
3 Exton Electrics has _____ a thousand new workers.
4 We can _____ the baby for the evening if you want to go out.
5 Perhaps you could _____ this letter for me, to check my spelling.
6 The manager promised to _____ my complaint.
7 Ken _____ his father: they both have a good head for business.
8 This summer Margaret's going to _____ tennis and join a club.
9 If our firm is _____ by a multinational company, I'll resign.
10 I tried to explain, but he didn't seem to _____ the news.

A Read the text and decide which word (A, B, C or D) best fits each space.

Revising for exams is not as easy as it looks. You will need to work out which routine suits you best, and 1) _____ stick to it. Some people like studying at night when it's quiet, whereas others find the early morning is a 2) _____ time to get things done. You might enjoy 3) _____ to music 4) _____ you revise, but this can be 5) _____ . Can you really concentrate 6) _____ two things at once? So think 7) _____ you turn your radio on!

Your 8) _____ is also important while you are revising. This may be a more than usually 9) _____ period of your life, when you 10) _____ take extra care to eat properly. No missed meals, or junk food, or 11) _____ cups of coffee! Get plenty of exercise as well. If you've got fed up with 12) _____ you're doing, or find it hard to concentrate, go for a walk to clear your head. 13) _____ exercise will help to keep your body fit and your brain working 14) _____ .

Finally, you also 15) _____ to take time off. Go out occasionally, see your friends, make time to relax. Then you will return to your studies fresh and full of enthusiasm!

	A	B	C	D
1	then	than	after	often
2	best	good	worse	well
3	to listen	having listened	listen	listening
4	during	while	however	throughout
5	unhelpful	helpful	helpless	helping
6	on	in	of	for
7	unless	if	before	after
8	slim	diet	healthy	menu
9	stressy	stressed	stressing	stressful
10	should	ought	need	might
11	worthless	hopeless	restless	endless
12	which	what	that	who
13	Strongly	Every	Regular	Always
14	well	energetic	good	correct
15	must	should	need	may

B Complete the passage, using one word for each space.

The Spanish painter Goya 1) _____ born in Aragon in 1746. Although very 2) _____ is known about his early 3) _____ , we do know 4) _____ he studied painting in his teens. He 5) _____ his artistic career by painting religious pictures 6) _____ wall-paintings for churches. 7) _____ 1773 he married 8) _____ woman 9) _____ three brothers were painters, and settled in Madrid.

There 10) _____ made sketches for the tapestries 11) _____ the Royal Tapestry Factory produced for the royal palaces. He also met a number of important 12) _____ whose portraits he painted. 13) _____ influence helped him become the 14) _____ fashionable painter 15) _____ Madrid society. 16) _____ most of his life Goya was the official painter of the Spanish royal family, 17) _____ in 1823 a change in Spanish politics 18) _____ him leave Spain. He went to France, 19) _____ he continued to paint. He died 20) _____ his home in Bordeaux in 1828.

C Complete the second sentence so that it has a similar meaning to the first one. Use between two and five words, including the word given. Do not change the word given.

1 He always gets his mother to wash his clothes.   HAS
He always _____ by his mother.

2 I advise you not to buy that car.   WERE
If _____ buy that car.

3 The town council is building a new football stadium.   BUILT
A new football stadium _____ the town council.

4 Paco doesn't dance as well as Pepe.   THAN
Pepe _____ Paco.

5 'Get on with your work!' the boss said to me.   TOLD
The boss _____ with my work.

6 Harold last went fishing two months ago.   BEEN
Harold _____ two months.

7 Could Alan stay with you for a couple of days?   PUT
Could you _____ for a couple of days?

8 One of Sally's favourite hobbies is windsurfing.   KEEN
Sally _____ windsurfing.

D Complete the sentences with the correct form of a phrasal verb with **bring** or **put.**

1 Would you please _____ your cigarette. This is a non-smoking compartment.

2 I'm sorry to have kept you waiting. I'm _____ you _____ to the manager now.

3 Jason's illness was _____ by a combination of overwork and poor diet.

4 They've redecorated the house and _____ central heating.

5 Pauline was _____ on a remote Scottish island, but later moved to the capital.

6 Publishers are _____ a lot of light novels for the holiday season.

7 Rupert _____ his trip to London because his father was taken ill.

8 He bought the television by _____ a deposit and then making monthly payments.

9 I'm worried about Paul. His freelance work only just _____ enough to pay the bills.

10 Campaigns by 'green' organizations have _____ a change in people's attitudes to the environment.

TEST 3

A Choose the correct word or phrase to complete each sentence. Write the letter in the space.

1 If it rains on Saturday, we shall have to _____ the match for a week.

   a) bring on   b) put away   c) take off   d) put off

2 I've lived near the airport for so long that I've got _____ to the noise of the planes.

   a) familiar   b) known   c) used   d) custom

3 She looks delighted – she _____ have received some good news.

   a) can   b) must   c) should   d) has to

4 I don't think that book is worth _____ .

   a) reading   b) read   c) to read   d) to reading

5 The quiz show was _____ two months after being recorded.

   a) emitted   b) sent out   c) broadcast   d) programmed

6 She always gets very good _____ in her exams.

   a) notes   b) marks   c) degrees   d) reports

7 David was brought _____ in the country by his grandparents.

   a) on   b) back   c) up   d) about

8 Experts are worried that _____ is damaging the ozone layer.

   a) pollution   b) chemicals   c) fumes   d) waste

9 Angela is engaged _____ Robert: their wedding is next month.

   a) with   b) to   c) by   d) for

10 She's starting a _____ today because she's rather overweight.

   a) slimming   b) regime   c) reduction   d) diet

11 He's taken his driving test five times, but he _____ it yet.

   a) hasn't passed   b) passed   c) didn't pass   d) is passing

12 There was _____ useful information in the newspaper report.

   a) any   b) a lot of   c) many   d) few

13 If only they _____ discuss their problems with each other more!

   a) will   b) would   c) were   d) might

14 The jury came back into court and gave their _____.

   a) sentence   b) guilty   c) evidence   d) verdict

15 If we _____ where you lived, we would have visited you.

   a) would have known   b) would know   c) had known
   d) have known

16 I had to pay the fine, _____ ?

   a) didn't I   b) hadn't I   c) wouldn't I   d) don't I

17 He won't be expecting a present, so you _____ buy him one.

   a) mustn't   b) have to   c) don't need   d) needn't

18 This soup _____ delicious. Why don't you try some?

   a) tasted   b) tastes   c) is tasting   d) has tasted

19 _____ who saw the robbery should contact the police.

   a) Somebody   b) One   c) Anyone   d) Someone

20 Fans often ask pop stars for their _____ .

   a) autograph   b) signature   c) handwriting   d) graphic

B Complete the passage, using one word for each space.

Serious damage to the ozone layer was 1) _____ detected over the Antarctic 2) _____ 1985. A recent survey, 3) _____ , shows that the ozone layer in the northern hemisphere could 4) _____ suffering similar 5) _____ . Scientists 6) _____ detected the highest levels 7) _____ recorded of ozone-destroying 8) _____ over North America 9) _____ Europe. The effect 10) _____ man-made chemicals has been made 11) _____ by the eruption of Mount Pinatubo 12) _____ the Philippines, which increased carbon monoxide 13) _____ in the upper atmosphere. It is 14) _____ that as many countries 15) _____ possible will sign an international treaty to 16) _____ and eventually halt the 17) _____ of chemicals like CFCs. If 18) _____ action 19) _____ taken, increased ultra-violet radiation could 20) _____ a large number of cases of skin cancer.

C Complete the second sentence so that it has a similar meaning to the first one. Use between two and five words, including the word given. Do not change the word given.

1 We've arranged for the office to be redecorated soon.   HAVING
   We're _____ soon.

2 The judge awarded Betty first prize in the contest.   WAS
   In the contest _____ by the judge.

3 James couldn't read the sign because he wasn't wearing his glasses.   IF
   James could have read the sign _____ his glasses.

4 Someone might want to see me – I'll be in the office.   CASE
   I'll be in the office _____ to see me.

5 He wanted to relax, so he took up yoga.   ORDER
   He took up yoga _____ relax.

6 Costas eats more fish than Sergio.   MUCH
   Sergio _____ fish as Costas.

7 They bought their cottage ten years ago.   FOR
   They _____ ten years.

8 I shall enjoy visiting my cousins next month.   FORWARD
   I'm _____ my cousins next month.

D Match each phrase or clause with the best ending. Write the letter next to the number on the right.

Now do the same for the rest of the exercise.

1 That morning we had to set	A in now.	1 ____
2 I'm not sure what I.T. stands	B out completely.	2 ____
3 Will you be able to stand	C for – do you know?	3 ____
4 It looks as if the bad weather has set	D in, if someone's ill?	4 ____
5 I'm afraid the coffee's run	E out before dawn.	5 ____
6 You'd better stand	F down your colleagues.	6 ____
7 I don't think you should run	G back by the spring frost.	7 ____
8 It was awful! She ran	H up for your rights!	8 ____
9 His vegetables were set	I out among the crowd.	9 ____
10 He was so tall that he stood	J over a rabbit yesterday.	10 ____

A Read the text and decide which word or phrase (A, B, C or D) best fits each space.

Anna Anderson, the woman who claimed for more 1) _____ sixty years, right up to her death in 1984, 2) _____ she was Grand Duchess Anastasia, 3) _____ youngest daughter of Tsar Nicholas II, 4) _____ been proved 5) _____ a fraud. 6) _____ many of Mrs Anderson's friends believed her story, forensic scientists 7) _____ carried out genetic tests on part of her intestine 8) _____ that she 9) _____ in fact a woman of Polish-German descent, who had disappeared in Berlin 10) _____ 1920, around the same time that Anna Anderson first appeared.

There is still no trace of Crown Prince Alexis or his sister Anastasia, 11) _____ bodies were missing from the communal grave of the Russian 12) _____ family, which was discovered in a forest in 1991. Researchers have offered no 13) _____ to the mystery so far. But despite the lack of clues, the public are still 14) _____ by the tragic death, or disappearance, of this young woman, and it seems 15) _____ that there will be continued interest in her story.

	A	B	C	D
1	then	as	less	than
2	that	so	and	when
3	a	the	one	another
4	is	was	has	had
5	to be	being	be	to being
6	Despite	In spite	Although	However
7	who	what	which	whose
8	tell	notice	say	inform
9	were	is	will be	was
10	in	on	at	while
11	their	whom	whose	of which
12	large	charming	famous	royal
13	solution	reason	background	system
14	fascinating	caring	fascinated	carefree
15	possibly	likelihood	maybe	probable

B Complete the passage, using one word for each space.

Ubar, 1) _____ of the great lost cities of the past, 2) _____ at last been found, 3) _____ in the sands of the Arabian desert 4) _____ Oman. For 2000 5) _____ Ubar was mentioned in travellers' tales and in many ancient 6) _____ . The city was 7) _____ as a world trading centre for spices and perfumes, with routes leading from it across 8) _____ desert 9) _____ Mesopotamia, Rome and Jerusalem. Archaeologists 10) _____ searched the desert for it several times, and 11) _____ of the great romantic explorers, including Lawrence of Arabia, had 12) _____ failed to find it. Ubar was 13) _____ discovered 14) _____ the infra-red cameras on the space shuttle Challenger 15) _____ photographs of the 16) _____ in 1984, revealing the ancient sand tracks used 17) _____ the camel caravans. At the centre of these 18) _____ archaeologists found the ruins of an 19) _____ city, which are thought to 20) _____ those of Ubar.

C Complete the second sentence so that it has a similar meaning to the first one. Use between two and five words, including the word given. Do not change the word given.

1 Has your lawyer received the documents yet?   BY
Have _____ your lawyer yet?

2 He gives orders all the time, which is very annoying.   HE
If _____ give orders all the time!

3 The old lady's gardener cut the grass for her yesterday.   HAD
The old lady _____ yesterday.

4 Jeff invited Rose to the theatre.   COME
'Would you _____ to the theatre with me, Rose?' said Jeff.

5 Don't shout like that – you'll wake the neighbours.   IF
You'll wake _____ like that.

6 It's possible that they have left the country.   MIGHT
They _____ the country.

7 The restaurant was often crowded, so she booked a table.   CASE
She booked a table _____ crowded.

8 Gary only complained because the service was poor.   BETTER
If the service _____, Gary wouldn't have complained.

D Complete the sentences with the correct form of a phrasal verb with **bring, set, stand** or **take.**

1 The company is thinking of _____ a new branch in the Middle East.

2 Talking about the past has _____ happy memories.

3 I _____ everything I said yesterday — I'm not withdrawing a single word.

4 You'd better _____ the information in your notebook, otherwise you'll forget it.

5 IGCSE _____ International General Certificate of Secondary Education.

6 Terence doesn't agree with me at the moment, but I'll soon _____ him _____ .

7 All the alarms were _____ when the downstairs window was broken.

8 Please _____ your dog _____ . Can't you see it's frightening my little girl?

9 Would anyone like to _____ any other points, before we close the meeting?

10 You may have to _____ for the chairman, and give the speech of welcome, if his flight is delayed.

TEST 5

A Some of the lines in this letter are correct, and others have a word which should not be there. Tick any lines which are correct. Write down any words which should not be there.

My friend Alexander is having a wonderful time at the
university. It's the freedom that he likes – he doesn't
live at the home, you see. Actually, he and his parents
didn't get on with well before he left home. They made
him to study for three hours every evening, gave him
a very little pocket-money, and didn't allow him to go out.
He's much more happier now, and goes out a lot with
his friends, in despite not having much money. He's
studying in London, and shares a flat with three another
boys in there. He doesn't always pass his exams, though,
and his teachers have told to him to study harder in
future. The problem is that he hasn't much time, because
of he has a part-time job to help pay the university fees.
He has no idea what kind of job to look for when he will
has finished his course, so he will probably do some
travelling and get seasonal or temporary work.

| 1 |
| 2 |
| 3 |
| 4 |
| 5 |
| 6 |
| 7 |
| 8 |
| 9 |
| 10 |
| 11 |
| 12 |
| 13 |
| 14 |
| 15 |
| 16 |

B Complete the text with adjectives or adverbs made from the words given in capitals.

The 1) _____ journal *The Economist* has discovered that
dustmen, whose 2) _____ job is to empty dustbins and
clear away rubbish, are 3) _____ at predicting Britain's
4) _____ situation than many cabinet ministers. Over a
ten-year period, dustmen gave more 5) _____ assessments
of current 6) _____ trends, as well as predictions for the
future, despite the fact that they are not 7) _____ in
economics, and earn much 8) _____ than ministers. *The
Economist* was 9) _____ by the results of its survey,
but 10) _____ refused to publish the names of ministers
who had performed so 11) _____.

POLITICS
USE
GOOD
ECONOMY
ACCURACY
NATION
TRAINING
LEAST
SURPRISE
CATEGORY
DISAPPOINT

C Complete the passage, using one word for each space.

Cheese has been part of our diet 1) _____ a very long time. As soon
2) _____ prehistoric man managed 3) _____ domesticate
4) _____ like cattle and sheep, he discovered how to 5) _____
cheese. In the ruins of prehistoric 6) _____ , cheese containers
7) _____ been found 8) _____ are similar to those used
9) _____ . So we can assume that cheese has always 10) _____
popular, and these days there is a great variety available. 11) _____
of it is mass-produced in factories. 12) _____ , you can still find tasty
farmhouse 13) _____ made from unpasteurised milk in the
traditional 14) _____ . Unfortunately it may 15) _____ become
illegal to sell this 16) _____ of cheese, if the European Union
17) _____ the use of unpasteurised 18) _____ in cheese. It
seems a pity 19) _____ such a long cheese-making tradition should
20) _____ to an end in this way.

D Complete the second sentence so that it has a similar meaning to the first one. Use between two and five words, including the word given. Do not change the word given.

1 You'd better get someone to sweep the chimney tomorrow.   HAVE
   You'd better _____ tomorrow.

2 Perhaps Fiona will come soon and then she'll be able to join us.   IF
   Fiona will be able to join us _____ soon.

3 To Amir's surprise his boss offered him promotion.   WAS
   To Amir's surprise _____ promotion.

4 Cars cost more in Britain than in Belgium.   MUCH
   Cars _____ in Belgium as in Britain.

5 'Where can I find the tourist office?' said Agnes.   COULD
   Agnes _____ the tourist office.

6 Although the weather was good, we stayed indoors.   DESPITE
   We stayed indoors _____ weather.

7 His ambition was to become the manager.   ALWAYS
   He _____ the manager.

8 It isn't necessary to eat all the food if you don't like it.   YOU
   If you don't like the food, _____ all of it.

E Complete the sentences with the correct form of a phrasal verb with **come** or **get**.

1 I _____ some old letters from Edmund the other day.

2 Gavin loved his job but could only just _____ on the low salary.

3 It took her a long time to _____ the accident.

4 Unfortunately his plan was too ambitious and didn't _____ .

5 Blackstone Road, please. Could you tell me which stop to _____ at.

6 It'll be marvellous to _____ from the office for a few days.

7 Something has _____ , so I'm afraid I'll have to miss the meeting.

8 I'm sure you can _____ the solution to the problem.

9 I'm not looking forward to my business trip. I wish I could _____ going.

10 They say the burglars _____ several valuable paintings.

11 How are you _____ with your project? The deadline's on Friday, isn't it?

12 You'll never persuade him! He'll never _____ to your way of thinking.

13 I think Nick will _____ quite a bit of money when his grandfather dies.

14 Bella Smith's new cookery book will be _____ soon – full of mouth-watering new recipes.

15 My uncle won't be able to come to the wedding. He's _____ a bit now, and can't travel far.

A Choose the correct word or phrase to complete each sentence. Write the letter in the space.

1 When he reached us, Henry was out of breath because he _____.
   a) ran   b) has run   c) had been running   d) was run

2 Do you think he's _____ to buy the stamps I asked him for?
   a) suggested   b) reminded   c) remembered   d) advised

3 So they're your favourite group. Have you ever seen them _____ ?
   a) alive   b) live   c) living   d) lively

4 I remember _____ round the exhibition a couple of years ago.
   a) being shown   b) to be shown   c) be shown   d) be showing

5 When she showed me the letter, I _____ her to throw it away.
   a) suggested   b) advised   c) informed   d) insisted

6 Passengers are asked _____ in rows A – G.
   a) don't smoke   b) not smoking   c) not to smoke   d) not smoke

7 The documents are _____ to be extremely valuable.
   a) said   b) told   c) described   d) spoken

8 Simon always _____ to do his homework before watching television.
   a) must   b) has   c) is having   d) is trying

9 The prisoner refused _____ the police with their enquiries.
   a) helping   b) help   c) to helping   d) to help

10 This _____ is best served with boiled rice and a crisp green salad.
   a) plate   b) meal   c) food   d) dish

11 The tourists refused to _____ the poor service.
   a) stand in for   b) get away from   c) put up with   d) get on with

12 By this time next year, I _____ my house.
   a) will sell   b) will have sold   c) have sold   d) sold

13 He's even worse than his sister _____ maths.
   a) at   b) with   c) in   d) for

14 Are there any _____ in your company for translators?
   a) spaces   b) vacancies   c) situations   d) offers

15 At first he didn't agree, but in the end we managed to bring him _____ to our point of view.
   a) up   b) over   c) round   d) back

16 People are becoming more and more interested in the _____ of wildlife and the environment.
   a) campaign   b) research   c) energy   d) conservation

17 The murderer was _____ to life imprisonment.
   a) sentenced   b) sent   c) judged   d) suspended

18 Since he started work, he _____ a mountain bike, a CD player and a computer.
   a) bought   b) is buying   c) has bought   d) buys

19 As I _____ down the road, I heard a woman scream.
   a) had walked   b) have walked   c) was walking   d) am walking

20 I'd be able to lead the way if you _____ me your map.
   a) lend   b) lent   c) are lending   d) will lend

B Complete the passage, using one word for each space.

Emile Zola, one of the 1) _____ known French novelists, was born in Paris in 1840. He 2) _____ a journalist, and he 3) _____ several collections of short stories. 4) _____ other writers he formed the Naturalist movement, 5) _____ encouraged writers 6) _____ use detailed realistic and factual description. Zola 7) _____ himself the technical details of 8) _____ professions and crafts, as well as the 9) _____ of recent events 10) _____ France. He put all this 11) _____ into his novels, which offer detailed descriptions of 12) _____ society. He 13) _____ wrote a series of twenty novels about 14) _____ same family, 15) _____ behaviour was strongly influenced 16) _____ their inherited characteristics. 17) _____ addition, Zola is 18) _____ for defending Alfred Dreyfus, who was accused 19) _____ spying, but was later proved 20) _____ . Zola died in Paris in 1902.

C Complete the second sentence so that it has a similar meaning to the first one. Use between two and five words, including the word given. Do not change the word given.

1 I'm sorry I forgot to ring you,' Mandy said.   APOLOGIZED
Mandy _____ to ring me.

2 Don't park there – ambulances need to use that space.   MUSTN'T
Ambulances need to use that space, so _____ there.

3 I might get thirsty, so I'll take some water with me.   CASE
I'll take some water with me, _____ thirsty.

4 Although he was tired, he was determined to finish his work.
SPITE
He was determined to finish his work _____ tired.

5 Not many fans came to support their team.   FEW
Only _____ to support their team.

6 Ann didn't take her passport, and realized it was a mistake.   HAD
Ann _____ her passport .

7 A violent storm almost destroyed the camp-site.   BY
The camp-site _____ a violent storm.

8 I'll take the film to be developed in town.   HAVE
I'll _____ in town.

D Complete the sentences with the correct form of a phrasal verb with **go** or **turn**.

1 Don't drink that milk. I think it's _____ .

2 That pink pullover doesn't really _____ those yellow trousers.

3 Guess who _____ last night? Your old friend Francisco!

4 It's cold in here now that the fire has _____ .

5 Can you _____ the television _____ a bit? It's far too loud.

6 That suggestion of his _____ very well with his boss.

7 The head waiter _____ us _____ because we hadn't booked a table.

8 After passing his French exam, he _____ to study German.

9 Christopher applied for the job, but they _____ him _____ .

10 You need a good friend to _____ when you're in trouble.

A Some of the lines in this letter are correct, and others have a word which should not be there. Tick any lines which are correct. Write down any words which should not be there.

A woman who fell ill on a holiday flight had got her life saved | 1
by two passengers, who happened to be the doctors. They | 2
carried out an emergency operation by with a coathanger, a | 3
bottle of mineral water, brandy and a knife and fork. Paula | 4
Dixon had been visiting to her sister in Hong Kong, and on the | 5
way to the airport for her flight home, she had been sudden | 6
involved in a road accident, and was more seriously injured | 7
than she has realized. She checked in and boarded the plane, | 8
but soon after it was took off, she felt ill and the cabin staff | 9
asked if there were any doctors on board. Fortunately, the two | 10
men who came forward, Professor Wallace and Dr Wong, both | 11
had an experience in treating accident victims. When Mrs | 12
Dixon had difficulty in for breathing, they knew her condition | 13
was serious and so she decided to perform an emergency | 14
operation. It was often successful, although the doctors | 15
admitted afterwards that they were afraid of it might not work. | 16
Mrs Dixon has now recovered completely and is extremely | 17
grateful to them.

B Complete the text with words made from the words given in capitals.

Getting around on holiday

Most people 1) _____ advise against hitchhiking   GENERAL
as it can be extremely 2) _____ . Walking or cycling   DANGER
are both very 3) _____ , and if you use your own bike,   HEALTH
very 4) _____ too. But perhaps you want to travel long   ECONOMY
5) _____ , or take a lot of luggage with you. In that   DISTANT
case, it is usually more 6) _____ to use your own car,   CONVENIENCE
or to hire one, although this can be 7) _____ . An   EXPENSE
environmentally-friendly 8) _____ is to use   SOLVE
public transport. This way you can 9) _____ the   APPRECIATION
countryside and meet people at the same time. Ask
for 10) _____ on ways of travelling from local   ADVISE
11) _____ offices.   TOUR

C Complete the passage, using one word for each space.

One of 1) _____ most romantic stories in British 2) _____ is that
of King Edward I and his Queen Eleanor, who 3) _____ in 1254,
when he was only 15 and she was 12. Eleanor 4) _____ a Spanish
princess, and Edward's father was King Henry III, 5) _____ gave the
young couple the countries of Ireland and Wales as a 6) _____
present. 7) _____ it was a political marriage, Edward and Eleanor
fell 8) _____ love, and 9) _____ when Edward went to war,
Eleanor was always at 10) _____ husband's side. They
11) _____ thirty-six contented years together, and 12) _____
Eleanor fell ill in Lincoln and died, Edward was never 13) _____ to

smile 14) _____ . Her funeral procession 15) _____ twelve days to make the 16) _____ from Lincoln to London. At every place 17) _____ the procession stopped each night, Edward 18) _____ a stone cross put up. The first of the Eleanor crosses is near Lincoln Castle, and the 19) _____ is at Charing Cross in London. They are the evidence of Edward's 20) _____ heart.

D Complete the second sentence so that it has a similar meaning to the first one. Use between two and five words, including the word given. Do not change the word given.

1 She plays so well that she's never lost a game.   A
  She's _____ she's never lost a game.
2 Dimitri hates people asking him for help.   OBJECTS
  Dimitri really _____ him for help
3 I'm pretty sure Celia has left the office.   HAVE
  Celia _____ the office.
4 Despite injuries to several players, the team won.   EVEN
  The team won, _____ injured.
5 'You stole my necklace!' the woman said to the boy.   STEALING
  The woman _____ her necklace.
6 Ingrid hasn't been skiing for five years.   LAST
  Ingrid _____ five years ago.
7 Jack wasn't allowed to play outside.   LET
  Jack's parents _____ outside.
8 By working hard, she managed to get a pay rise.   GETTING
  By working hard, she _____ a pay rise.
9 The workers are on strike because of low pay.   MORE
  If the workers _____ , they wouldn't be on strike.

E Match each phrase or clause with the best ending. Write the letter next to the number on the right.

Now do the same for the rest of the exercise.

1	Will you be seeing	A	down on the motorway.	1 ____
2	Have you tried to give	B	to the arrangements for you.	2 ____
3	The removal van broke	C	him off at the airport?	3 ____
4	I can see	D	out following the government's collapse.	4 ____
5	Civil war broke	E	up smoking?	5 ____
6	She always sees	F	in and admit defeat.	6 ____
7	Negotiations were broken	G	through his feeble excuses.	7 ____
8	The champion was forced to give	H	off their engagement.	8 ____
9	She gave back the ring and broke	I	out of prison in a helicopter.	9 ____
10	Some of the bank robbers broke	J	off after two weeks.	10 ____

TEST 8

A Choose the correct word or phrase to complete each sentence. Write the letter in the space.

1 I haven't been out much lately, because I _____ for my exams.

    a) studied   b) have been studying   c) have studied   d) had studied

2 Fiona is used to _____ late at the office.

    a) work   b) have worked   c) working   d) being worked

3 He was offered the job _____ he had no experience.

    a) even though   b) despite   c) while   d) however

4 It's no use _____ lies. They'll find out the truth in the end.

    a) tell   b) told   c) to tell   d) telling

5 The three men were _____ with robbing a bank.

    a) arrested   b) accused   c) charged   d) judged

6 I _____ my brother to enter the competition.

    a) warned   b) suggested   c) encouraged   d) said

7 Philip went to Jordan hoping to find a teaching _____ .

    a) work   b) post   c) employment   d) occupation

8 We shall dismiss you unless your work _____ by the end of the month.

    a) will improve   b) improves   c) would improve   d) improved

9 I didn't see Diane at the party, so she _____ have been there.

    a) mustn't   b) wasn't   c) shouldn't   d) can't

10 Pierre can't stand _____ to wait.

    a) be made   b) to be made   c) being made   d) be making

11 You can use the card to _____ cash from your account at any time.

    a) withdraw   b) pay   c) earn   d) spend

12 Doctors can now offer _____ for certain types of cancer.

    a) antidote   b) cure   c) treatment   d) hospital

13 There were only _____ people waiting in the queue.

    a) a little   b) many   c) not a lot   d) a few

14 We had an exciting _____ on the Trans-Siberian railway.

    a) travel   b) trip   c) tour   d) cruise

15 He wishes he _____ harder for his exams.

    a) has studied   b) would study   c) studies   d) had studied

16 Scientists are carrying out a number of _____ into ways of improving technology in the home.

    a) experiments   b) research   c) progress   d) inventions

17 He'll have to wait there until the ambulance _____ .

    a) will arrive   b) would arrive   c) arrives   d) is arriving

18 Laura _____ to ring me back as soon as she could.

    a) suggested   b) informed   c) apologized   d) promised

19 The couple invited all their relatives and friends to their _____.

    a) marriage   b) wedding   c) ceremony   d) engagement

20 When Steve retired, he decided to take _____ badminton.

    a) on   b) up   c) over   d) out

B Complete the passage, using one word for each space.

Cleopatra, Queen of Egypt, was 1) _____ to be the most beautiful woman 2) _____ the world. The Roman Emperor, Julius Caesar, 3) _____ in love with her, and by helping her to 4) _____ a war against her brother Ptolemy, established her authority 5) _____ Egypt. 6) _____ a time Cleopatra lived with Julius Caesar in Rome, 7) _____ when he was murdered she 8) _____ to Egypt. Soon afterwards she met the great Roman general, Mark Antony, 9) _____ was fascinated 10) _____ her astonishing beauty. He 11) _____ most of his time at Cleopatra's palace in Alexandria, 12) _____ the couple lived in luxury and idleness. Because of this, Mark Antony 13) _____ his popularity in Rome, and in the end he 14) _____ defeated in the sea battle of Actium by another Roman general. When he heard news 15) _____ Cleopatra was dead, he knew he had 16) _____ to live for, and he tried to kill himself. 17) _____, the information was false and 18) _____ Mark Antony was carried to Cleopatra's 19) _____ , he died in her arms. Unable to live 20) _____ him, she killed herself immediately afterwards.

C Complete the second sentence so that it has a similar meaning to the first one. Use between two and five words, including the word given. Do not change the word given.

1 There isn't much water in the river bed this summer.   VERY
   There _____ in the river bed this summer.

2 During her conversation with her mother she was cut off.   SHE
   She was cut off _____ her mother.

3 'Can I help you with those bags?' Ken said to the girl.   TO
   Ken _____ with her bags.

4 That's the most delicious fish I've ever tasted.   NEVER
   I've _____ fish.

5 Roy's boss didn't let him have a holiday last year.   ALLOWED
   Roy _____ a holiday last year.

6 He ought to get a job and settle down.   GOT
   It's _____ a job and settled down.

7 Ali refused the invitation and then regretted it.   WISHED
   Ali _____ the invitation.

8 We will do everything possible to avoid a disaster.   BE
   Everything possible _____ to avoid a disaster.

D Complete the sentences with the correct form of a phrasal verb with **break**, **get**, **give** or **turn**.

1 Everyone _____ well with the receptionist – she's so friendly.

2 The pilot had to _____ to the airport because of a faulty engine.

3 He was determined to _____ his son _____ a top athlete.

4 You'll have to _____ eating so many sweets, or you'll have trouble with your teeth.

5 The police think the burglars _____ through the cloakroom window.

6 When my neighbour won the National Lottery, he _____ half the money _____ to charity.

7 The meeting _____ on the stroke of midnight.

8 I suppose one day we'll _____ repairing the greenhouse – it just isn't a priority.

IRREGULAR VERBS

Infinitive	Past Simple	Past Participle	Infinitive	Past Simple	Past Participle
be	was/were	been	learn	learnt, learned	learnt, learned
beat	beat	beaten	leave	left	left
become	became	become	lend	lent	lent
begin	began	begun	let	let	let
bend	bent	bent	lie	lay	lain
bite	bit	bitten	lose	lost	lost
blow	blew	blown			
break	broke	broken	make	made	made
bring	brought	brought	mean	meant	meant
build	built	built	meet	met	met
burn	burnt, burned	burnt, burned			
buy	bought	bought	pay	paid	paid
			put	put	put
catch	caught	caught			
choose	chose	chosen	read	read	read
come	came	come	ride	rode	ridden
cost	cost	cost	ring	rang	rung
cut	cut	cut	rise	rose	risen
			run	ran	run
do	did	done			
draw	drew	drawn	say	said	said
dream	dreamt, dreamed	dreamt, dreamed	see	saw	seen
drink	drank	drunk	sell	sold	sold
drive	drove	driven	send	sent	sent
			shake	shook	shaken
eat	ate	eaten	shine	shone	shone
			shoot	shot	shot
fall	fell	fallen	show	showed	shown, showed
feed	fed	fed	shut	shut	shut
feel	felt	felt	sing	sang	sung
fight	fought	fought	sink	sank	sunk
find	found	found	sit	sat	sat
fly	flew	flown	sleep	slept	slept
forget	forgot	forgotten	smell	smelt, smelled	smelt, smelled
freeze	froze	frozen	speak	spoke	spoken
			spend	spent	spent
get	got	got	stand	stood	stood
give	gave	given	steal	stole	stolen
go	went	gone	stick	stuck	stuck
grow	grew	grown	strike	struck	struck
			swim	swam	swum
hang	hung	hung			
have	had	had	take	took	taken
hear	heard	heard	teach	taught	taught
hide	hid	hidden	tear	tore	torn
hit	hit	hit	tell	told	told
hold	held	held	think	thought	thought
hurt	hurt	hurt	throw	threw	thrown
keep	kept	kept	understand	understood	understood
know	knew	known			
			wake	woke	woken
lay	laid	laid	wear	wore	worn
lead	led	led	win	won	won
lean	leant, leaned	leant, leaned	write	wrote	written

KEY

Unit 1

A 1 eats
2 'm helping
3 aren't studying
4 drink
5 goes
6 is having
7 are making
8 smoke
9 washes
10 is driving
11 flows
12 fly

B 1 Do you speak Greek?
2 Does Bill know Mr Jameson?
3 We don't live in a large house.
4 Alexander doesn't go to the beach very often.
5 Do I have to attend the ceremony?
6 Is Jane watching television at the moment?
7 Costas doesn't work in a bank.
8 The children aren't listening to their mother now.
9 Does Theo live in New York?
10 Is William studying at the moment?
11 Where do you usually spend your holidays?
12 I'm not earning much money at present.

C 1 is appearing
2 prefers
3 appears
4 is thinking
5 belongs
6 believes
7 hates
8 tastes
9 seems
10 understand, means
11 smells
12 owes

D 1 works, isn't working
2 is running, is carrying
3 cries
4 takes, shakes, look
5 am helping
6 drives, is driving
7 live, am studying, am living
8 aren't listening, are looking
9 speaks, is working
10 wear, feel
11 floats
12 are you crying, loves

Unit 2

A 1 went
2 has lent
3 drove away
4 closed down
5 has been lying
6 has just passed
7 has been studying
8 came
9 has been trying
10 has already told
11 hasn't taken
12 have left
13 fell
14 have just had
15 have forgotten

B 1 When did you last go to Spain?
2 Have you ever spoken to a film star?
3 Did you spend a lot of money last month?
4 I haven't said anything up to now.
5 Laura hasn't had a holiday so far this year.
6 Have you seen any good films lately?
7 Have you ever been to Japan?
8 Has Helmut written to you yet?
9 Did the boys finish their homework yesterday?
10 Rolf didn't buy the leather jacket last week.

C 1 for
2 since
3 for
4 Since
5 for
6 for
7 since
8 for
9 since
10 for

D 1 have died
2 crashed
3 was
4 saw
5 alerted
6 rushed
7 have been working
8 have just managed
9 has already taken
10 have not released
11 has sentenced
12 told
13 (had) stopped
14 wanted
15 found
16 asked
17 decided
18 sent

Unit 3

A 1 was getting
2 was shining
3 was snowing
4 was reading
5 were singing

B 1 was watching, rang

2 was having, arrived

3 broke, was skiing

4 was listening, heard

5 fell, was climbing

6 were giving, arrived

7 was waiting, noticed

8 decided, was raining

9 stole, was looking

10 was crossing, crashed

C 1B   2A   3F   4C   5D   6E

Unit 4

A 1 had sold

2 had been studying

3 had fallen over

4 had arranged

5 had already bought

6 had been saving up/had saved up

7 had already seen

8 had been

B 1 had finished, went

2 arrived, had already gone out

3 left, said

4 doing/he had done, went out

5 reached, phoned

6 had run, felt

C 1 Before Dora did the shopping,…

2 ✔

3 ✔

4 … his father bought him a car.

5 I only put a match to it …

6 ✔

7 … because I've been running …

Unit 5

A 1 b   4 a

2 a   5 c

3 d   6 b

7 d   14 b

8 a   15 a

9 c   16 c

10 b   17 d

11 c   18 c

12 d   19 b

13 a   20 a

B 1 haven't been shopping for

2 went to Greece for/on

3 have been waiting here for

4 ages since I've

5 arrived, the burglar had

6 Fred was painting a wall

7 had finished when Mr Jenkins

8 see the doctor after making

9 before inviting

10 was raining heavily as

C 1 has   9 was

2 ago   10 ✔

3 ✔   11 have

4 been   12 to

5 being   13 were

6 not   14 ✔

7 be   15 ✔

8 already

Unit 6

A 1 If the sun shines, we'll go for a walk.

2 People cannot ski in the Alps if there is no snow.

3 Unless Isabelle runs, she won't catch the bus.

4 You'll be able to drive my car if you pass your driving test.

5 Unless you go to bed early, you'll be tired tomorrow.

6 Ice always melts if the air temperature is warm enough.

7 I won't sign the contract unless you agree to it.

8 If you have time, you'll be able to visit the exhibition.

B 1 if I won

2 working, I wouldn't feel

3 gave up smoking, he/it would

4 went to Arizona, I could

5 were you, I would revise

6 spoke Spanish better/better Spanish, I could

C 1 wouldn't have had, had driven/had been driving

2 hadn't lent, wouldn't have bought

3 would have sent, had reminded

4 had slept, wouldn't be

5 would have caught, had got

D 1 Before you leave Athens, you must visit the Parthenon.

2 When he comes home, he'll get his supper.

3 While you're on holiday, I'll water your plants for you.

4 As soon as the programme finishes, I'll switch off the television.

5 I'll go on applying for jobs until I get one.

6 After I've had a shower, I'll cook the dinner.

E 1 use/have flour, you can't

2 had some money, we could

3 gets better, I'll be

4 hadn't eaten so much

5 had noticed him, I would

6 unless somebody rings the

Unit 7

A 1 The prizegiving is held in the hall every year.

2 All the power cables have been brought down by a storm.

3 The price of gas was raised last year by the government.

4 All the arrangements were made for the President's visit.

5 Had she been invited before last weekend?

6 Her passport is being renewed next week.

7 Blocks of flats are being built all over the town by the authorities.

8 The theft has not been investigated by the police yet.

9 The contract was signed by the two businessmen.

10 The bottles will be collected for recycling.

11 The new theatre is being opened by the Mayor on Saturday.

12 The cows were being milked when I arrived at the farm.

B 1 be arrested/have been arrested
2 be brought up
3 be paid
4 be denied
5 to be painted
6 be built
7 be done
8 be parked
9 have been looked after
10 be cleaned
11 be sent for
12 be taken on

C 1 a 6 b
2 b 7 b
3 b 8 a
4 b 9 a
5 a 10 b

D 1 I don't mind being given presents!
2 Charlotte hates being treated like a baby.
3 He's used to his English being corrected.

4 I don't enjoy being made to do the washing-up.

5 I can't stand being ignored.

6 He doesn't remember being punished at school.

7 I'm looking forward to being sent abroad by my company.

8 My dog simply loves being taken for a walk.

9 You'll never forget being taught by your very first teacher.

10 Yesterday I spent two hours being shown how to use the computer.

E 1 The invitations were sent a fortnight before the wedding.

2 I hope my passport will be stamped by the airport officials.

3 No newspapers were delivered at number 25 last week.

4 The problem cannot be solved without the government's help.

5 The match had to be cancelled when rain flooded the pitch.

6 The results of the experiments will be published in leading scientific journals.

7 He was presented with a large cheque at his retirement party.

8 All travel arrangements must be completed by 17th June/June 17th.

Unit 8

A 1 is reported to have
2 that the Prime Minister is
3 are believed to have been
4 that football is
5 said that diamonds are
6 is known to have
7 is understood to be
8 is supposed to be

B 1 It is said that we'll run out of oil one day.

2 It was reported that no witnesses had come forward ... / No witnesses were reported to have come forward...

3 This is considered a wonderful opportunity for young people.

4 It is (generally) believed that the solution to the mystery will never be discovered.

5 He is considered guilty by his lawyer.

6 It is thought that the local cinema will close down soon.

7 It is (widely) known that the Robinson family moved away last week. / The Robinson family are (widely) known to have moved away last week.

8 It is said that we should eat more fruit and vegetables.

9 It is reported that prices are rising in Paris. / Prices are reported to be rising in Paris.

10 It is understood that Stuart won't be in the team this season.

11 It is thought the weather will improve next week.

12 It is known that the British Isles were once part ... / The British Isles are known to have once been part ...

Unit 9

A 1 isn't it? 7 are we?
2 doesn't he? 8 could you?
3 have you? 9 is she?
4 will he? 10 do you?
5 didn't she? 11 can't we?
6 wasn't it? 12 has he?

B 1 wouldn't he?
2 will you?
3 hadn't they?
4 aren't I?

5 shall we?

6 will you?

7 wouldn't you?

8 shall we?

9 had they?

10 didn't she?

Unit 10

A 1 a   11 c

2 d   12 d

3 b   13 b

4 a   14 c

5 a   15 a

6 b   16 d

7 d   17 d

8 c   18 b

9 b   19 c

10 a   20 a

B 1 was still being baked

2 when he graduates

3 did they start (doing)

4 could not be typed

5 did any/some gardening was

6 hadn't broken her leg

7 has been awarded

8 unless we can get

C 1 enjoying   9 some

2 will   10 did

3 ✔   11 are

4 been   12 was

5 had   13 be

6 ✔   14 being

7 ✔   15 been

8 had   16 ✔

Unit 11

A 1 Elisa said (that) she was going to London the following week.

2 The teacher said (that) he spoke very good German.

3 Philip's wife said (that) she came from Izmir.

4 The policewoman said (that) he had broken out of prison the day before.

5 Ursula said (that) she had just passed her driving test.

6 The guide said (that) they were building a museum in the main square.

7 Mrs Hall said (that) she would help Joe as much as she could.

8 Maria said (that) she worked eight hours a day, except when the children were on holiday.

9 Michael said (that) he hadn't seen Bridget for ages.

10 Rosemary said (that) she thought she had forgotten to lock the door that morning.

B 1 came, would give

2 wouldn't have laughed, had known

3 would help, could

4 paid, would call

5 wouldn't have fallen, had been

6 would be, won

7 wouldn't have had, hadn't been

8 wouldn't have lost, had worked

C 1 'Would you like to come to the cinema (with me), Sam?' asked Mark.

2 'Why don't we all go to the beach? / Let's all go to the beach,' said Pierre.

3 'If I were you, I'd tell the truth,' said Zoraya.

4 'Go on, Tom, you can mend it!' said Susanne.

5 'I'm sorry I'm late,' said Jeff.

6 'You stole my bike, Roy!' said Gabriela.

7 'I didn't take the book,' said Erika.

8 'Yes, I broke the window,' said Alberto.

9 'You should try the pasta,' the waiter told us.

10 'Nicole, don't forget to phone your mother,' said the teacher.

D 1 Lilian asked Pat if/whether she could see her the next/the following day.

2 David asked John who he thought would win.

3 Peter asked Mr Black how much he owed him.

4 Jane asked Elena when she had last seen Carlos.

5 Vera asked Roger if/whether he had ever been to Delphi.

6 Chantal asked Donald if/whether he would be around on Friday.

7 Michelle asked why he hadn't come/been to school.

8 Daniela asked if/whether Jonathan liked steak.

9 Sally asked if/whether they had arrived on time.

10 Ali's mother asked him where he had been all morning.

E 1 Liz told the boy not to do that.

2 The manager asked the ladies/women to take a seat.

3 The air hostess asked the passengers not to smoke in those seats.

4 The teacher asked Tricia to open the window.

5 The man told the driver to go up the road and take the first left.

6 The bank robber told the clerk to hand over the money.

7 Diana told them all to leave her alone.

8 Bill asked Sheila to give him a lift to the airport.

9 Mr Harrap told his secretary to type those letters first.

10 Mark asked Patrick to lend him £10.

F 1 admitted
   2 apologized
   3 encouraged
   4 suggested
   5 denied
   6 advised
   7 asked
   8 accused
   9 warned
  10 recommended

Unit 12

A 1 would   5 would
   2 could   6 could
   3 could   7 would
   4 could   8 could

B 1 I had more/a lot of
   2 she were/was far away
   3 didn't live so far
   4 only I didn't have
   5 I were better at
   6 didn't live in
   7 only I knew how
   8 it didn't rain

C 1 hadn't been
   2 had driven
   3 had found
   4 had known
   5 hadn't broken
   6 hadn't written
   7 had left
   8 hadn't bought
   9 had understood
  10 hadn't attacked

D 1 wishes he hadn't smashed
   2 she hadn't left
   3 wish I had
   4 only the snow would
   5 wish we had brought
   6 wish I were/was lying
   7 only I hadn't spent
   8 wish he wouldn't/didn't talk
   9 only I could go

  10 only I had studied harder
  11 only Pablo would phone me
  12 wish we were

Unit 13

A 1 I'm visiting my cousin in Paris.
   2 Are you flying?
   3 'm going by coach.
   4 What time does it leave?
   5 'll send you a postcard.

B 1 arrives
   2 won't like
   3 is going to study
   4 'm visiting/'m going to visit
   5 's going to rain
   6 're going to be/'ll be
   7 'll open
   8 'm going to work
   9 aren't going to hire/aren't hiring
  10 will you be
  11 Will you let
  12 'll phone
  13 Shall I help
  14 'm going to see
  15 will be

Unit 14

A 1 I'll be wearing
   2 won't be waiting
   3 he'll (still) be writing
   4 Ben will be driving
   5 Fatima will be doing
   6 won't be watching

B 1 will have been
   2 will have finished
   3 will have produced
   4 will have typed
   5 will have driven
   6 will have passed
   7 won't have finished
   8 Will you have finished

C 1 will you be doing
   2 'll be studying
   3 'll be teaching
   4 'll have finished
   5 won't see
   6 'll probably have got married
   7 had
   8 'll have discovered

Unit 15

A 1 d   11 c
   2 c   12 a
   3 a   13 b
   4 c   14 a
   5 b   15 c
   6 a   16 d
   7 d   17 a
   8 c   18 b
   9 b   19 b
  10 d   20 c

B 1 me to be careful
   2 has never been
   3 had asked her, she would
   4 is often played
   5 Susan where she had
   6 invited Jim to a
   7 my father will have
   8 I am flying/am going to fly

C 1B   2C   3D   4A   5C   6A
   7B   8C   9A   10D   11B
   12A   13C   14B

Unit 16

A 1 on   9 on
   2 in   10 on
   3 at   11 at
   4 in   12 on
   5 in   13 at
   6 in   14 at
   7 in   15 at
   8 at   16 at

B 1C   2G   3D   4J   5B   6I
   7A   8F   9E   10H

C 1 to   9 for
2 ✔   10 to
3 from   11 ✔
4 with   12 about
5 on   13 was
6 ✔   14 ✔
7 to   15 them
8 the

D 1 for   6 for
2 with   7 at
3 with   8 to
4 about   9 to
5 of   10 of

Unit 17

A 1 easier, than
2 bigger than
3 more slowly than
4 more important than
5 more comfortable than
6 more peaceful than
7 more beautiful than
8 longer than

B 1 drink as much milk as
2 better than
3 isn't as tall as
4 lives further/farther (away) from Tokyo
5 doesn't have as many
6 typing is worse than

C 1 the largest
2 the most beautiful
3 the most expensive
4 the easiest
5 the worst
6 the most difficult
7 the most popular
8 the richest

D 1 has never had such a
2 the worst driver in
3 ever said such a hurtful
4 first time I've (ever)
5 the best coffee I've
6 is the most interesting

7 a more generous person than/ anyone more generous than
8 is as cheap as that

Unit 18

A 1E   2D   3B   4F   5C   6A

B 1 had it made
2 had it cut
3 having it repaired
4 have it serviced
5 have them cleaned
6 have it installed
7 having it fitted
8 have them mended
9 have it X-rayed
10 have them checked

C 1 Sue had her hair washed by the hairdresser.
2 ✔
3 ✔
4 Robert is going to have his car serviced by the local mechanic.
5 They're having the trees cut down by the workmen.
6 ✔
7 I couldn't understand the letter, so I had it translated.
8 He had his photo taken by a famous photographer.
9 ✔
10 ✔

Unit 19

A 1 a   9 the
2 a   10 the
3 a   11 the
4 the   12 the
5 a   13 a
6 the   14 the
7 The   15 the
8 the   16 a

B 1 –   5 the
2 the, the   6 –
3 –, –   7 –
4 the   8 –

9 the, the   12 the
10 –   13 the
11 –   14 –

Unit 20

A 1 a   11 a
2 d   12 a
3 c   13 d
4 c   14 c
5 b   15 d
6 a   16 a
7 b   17 b
8 d   18 c
9 c   19 a
10 b   20 d

B 1 don't approve of her coming
2 is supposed to be
3 apologized for being/ arriving
4 isn't as intelligent as
5 most beautiful sunset I have
6 had his CD player
7 had known he was rich
8 wished he had (some)

C 1 will   7 summer
2 to   8 the
3 been   9 a
4 more   10 ✔
5 buy/like   11 at
6 One/another   12 a

Unit 21

A 1 will let him leave
2 was made to join
3 is allowed to get up
4 were made to do
5 let me vote
6 didn't let Duncan join
7 make the student
8 am not allowed to smoke

B 1 does/did   5 done
2 makes   6 made
3 done   7 do
4 do   8 make

C 1D 2G 3A 4H 5F 6C
7E 8B

D 1 used to swim
2 got used to queu(e)ing
3 used to eating
4 used to travel
5 used to listen
6 get used to
7 used to watch
8 used to getting up
9 use to live
10 use to like

Unit 22

A 1 who   6 who
2 what   7 what
3 which/that   8 whose
4 where   9 which/that
5 whose   10 who

B 1 She put on the clothes she had bought the day before.
2 I wanted to see the man who owned the restaurant.
3 There are lots of interesting places I'd like to visit.
4 That's the boy my brother plays basketball with.
5 I'm looking forward to the programme which/that is on after the news.
6 Do you remember the hotel in Edinburgh where your parents stayed last year?
7 Those are the shoes I cleaned for you.
8 He's written down the word he looked up yesterday.
9 That's the old lady whose brother won the Nobel Prize.
10 I've lost the list I had in my hand a moment ago.

C 1 He gave me the information, which I wrote down at once.
2 Andrea went to see the dentist, who took out two of her teeth.
3 Fritz lives in the house round the corner, which has a red front door.
4 Show me the shoes (which/that) you bought yesterday.
5 Have you seen the film which/that is on at the Odeon?
6 My boyfriend, who hates country music, refused to go to the concert with me.
7 We climbed to the top of the mountain, where we had a picnic.
8 Edward, whose mother died last year, has just moved to France.
9 We didn't want to swim in the sea, which looked very dirty.
10 Lydia is reading that fascinating book on Spanish history (which/that) you lent her last week.

D 1 is nothing you can do
2 best film about love that
3 ate all the food which/that
4 biggest dog I've ever
5 produced by the company have
6 everything that/which has been

Unit 23

A 1 some
2 any
3 anywhere
4 Somebody/Someone
5 any
6 any
7 some
8 something
9 anybody/anyone
10 any
11 anything
12 somewhere
13 Somebody/Someone
14 Anybody/Anyone

B *Uncountable:* furniture, news, knowledge, information, meat, money, milk, cheese, water, luggage, butter, advice

C 1 a lot of   6 much
2 much   7 little
3 a little   8 a lot of
4 many   9 Few
5 a few   10 many

D 1 any   7 some
2 a lot of   8 a lot of
3 a little   9 a little
4 many   10 a few
5 a few   11 any
6 much   12 very little

E 1B 2C 3D 4E 5A
6I 7F 8J 9H 10G

Unit 24

A 1 eating   11 talking
2 asking   12 to play
3 swimming   13 to pass
4 to work   14 arriving
5 to help   15 going
6 going   16 stealing
7 learning   17 spending
8 hitting   18 getting
9 being   19 telling
10 deceiving   20 to travel

B 1 to invite
2 to repair
3 painting
4 seeing
5 going
6 to have
7 explaining
8 holding, drinking
9 to pay
10 Collecting
11 driving
12 being
13 to get
14 to find
15 running

C 1 Pedro enjoys having …
2 ✔
3 Sylvie spent three weeks revising …
4 These shoes need mending, …
5 We encouraged him to apply …
6 ✔
7 He risked offending her …
8 ✔
9 ✔
10 Would you consider working …

Unit 25

A 1 c 11 b
2 d 12 d
3 a 13 a
4 a 14 c
5 b 15 a
6 c 16 b
7 d 17 d
8 b 18 c
9 c 19 a
10 a 20 c

B 1 spent four hours doing
2 tends to go away
3 I were you, I'd
4 a few people were
5 promised to give the money
6 never allowed to stay
7 looking forward to seeing
8 have those shoes mended

C 1A 2B 3C 4B 5A 6C
7C 8B 9A 10D 11C
12A 13D 14B

Unit 26

A 1 his (great) age
2 I studied hard
3 of the fact that
4 though I told her to
5 doing well

B 1 gets   4 turn up
2 rains 5 tried
3 went

C 1 for me to go to
2 Bianca did some
3 he got
4 for us to say
5 you posted those

D 1B 2E 3A 4H 5G 6D
7C

Unit 27

A 1 have   5 ought
2 should 6 can
3 may   7 be able
4 must

B 1B 2D 3E 4C 5A

C 1 mustn't   4 mustn't
2 needn't 5 needn't
3 needn't

D 1 can't be
2 must have left
3 must be
4 may/might be
5 must have cost
6 can't have booked
7 may/might have made
8 must be

E 1 I was able to/managed to climb … / succeeding in climbing …
2 Did you manage to finish …
3 ✔
4 … were able to/managed to put out …/ succeeded in putting out …
5 The pupils succeeding in collecting …
6 ✔

7 ✔
8 ✔

Unit 28

A 1 professional
2 practical
3 doubtful
4 commercial
5 hopeful
6 successful
7 scientific
8 personal
9 lucky
10 endless
11 variable

B 1 angrily
2 comfortable
3 wonderful
4 easily
5 thoughtfully
6 sad
7 carefully
8 excellent

C 1 amused
2 boring
3 terrifying
4 disgusted
5 frightened
6 thrilling
7 interested

Unit 29

A 1 early
2 elegantly
3 late
4 hard
5 politely
6 efficiently
7 legally
8 highly
9 fast
10 methodically
11 Unfortunately
12 suddenly

B 1 I often go to the cinema.
2 We do our homework every day.
3 I like melon and strawberries very much.
4 Andreas drove the car as fast as possible.
5 ✔
6 Suddenly the police entered ... / The police suddenly entered ...
7 The students passed the exam with a grade C.
8 The grass was occasionally cut .../was cut occasionally...
9 They have always attended this school.
10 ✔

Unit 30

A 1G 2C 3F 4E 5B 6A
7I 8D

B 1 won't be able to/'m not able to
2 have to sign
3 (really) ought to take him
4 (often) used to play/would often play
5 may not be
6 mustn't be so rude
7 the pool needs cleaning
8 needn't (bother to) lock

C 1 the
2 most
3 Although
4 there
5 was
6 by
7 about
8 need
9 because/as/since
10 not/hardly
11 that
12 more
13 in
14 these
15 time/necessary/important/ vital

16 recently/newly/just
17 should
18 better/more/increased/ improved
19 lower/cheaper
20 will

D 1 exciting
2 accurately
3 speedily
4 highly
5 enthusiastic
6 professional
7 residential
8 daily
9 available
10 incredibly
11 attractive
12 interested
13 immediately

Unit 31

A 1 Look out
2 looking into
3 looked round
4 looking for
5 look through
6 look, up
7 looks, like
8 looking at
9 looked down on
10 looking forward to
11 looked on
12 looking after

B 1 looked up to
2 looks like
3 take care of
4 look for
5 looked down on

C 1 up   4 at
2 into   5 for
3 after

Unit 32

A 1 takes off
2 taking, out
3 took down
4 takes after
5 take up
6 take back
7 taken over
8 take, in
9 took on
10 take out
11 Take, away
12 take, up

B 1B 2A 3D 4C 5H 6E
7F 8G

C 1 off   4 on
2 in   5 back
3 up

Unit 33

A 1 put, out
2 put up with
3 put in
4 put off
5 putting, through
6 put on
7 put down
8 put, up
9 Put, away
10 put forward
11 put on
12 put off

B 1 put Tim up
2 is putting on
3 put off
4 put out
5 putting forward
6 putting you through
7 putting in
8 put away
9 put up with
10 put off

C 1 off   4 out
    2 down   5 up
    3 on

Unit 34

A 1 brought up
    2 brought on
    3 bringing out
    4 bring, round
    5 brings back
    6 brings in
    7 bring about
    8 bring down
    9 bring up
    10 brought in
    11 bring, round
    12 brought down

B 1D   2C   3A   4E   5B   6H
    7I   8J   9F   10G

Unit 35

A 1B   2F   3H   4C   5E   6D
    7A   8G   9I   10J

B 1 stands
    2 sets
    3 sets
    4 stand
    5 runs
    6 away
    7 setting/drawing
    8 down

C 1B   2E   3A   4C   5D

Unit 36

A 1F   2T   3F   4F   5F   6T
    7F   8T

B 1 b   4 c
    2 a   5 b
    3 d   6 d

C 1 looks like
    2 look

    3 put
    4 taken away
    5 brought
    6 out!

D 1E   2A   3B   4C   5D   6H
    7F   8I   9J   10G

E 1 out   7 forward
    2 takes   8 at
    3 brought   9 for
    4 up   10 put
    5 in   11 forward
    6 looking

F 1B   2A   3C   4A   5A   6D
    7C   8A   9B

Unit 37

A 1 came across
    2 came out
    3 come down with
    4 comes to
    5 came up with
    6 come up
    7 came round
    8 came off
    9 came down
    10 Come on
    11 come in
    12 come back
    13 came into
    14 come off
    15 came round

B 1C   2A   3E   4B   5D   6H
    7J   8G   9F   10I

Unit 38

A 1 go by
    2 went down
    3 go for
    4 go into
    5 go away
    6 went out/off
    7 going out
    8 went through

    9 gone off
    10 went up
    11 go with
    12 went on
    13 going on
    14 go over/through
    15 Go on

B 1C   2D   3B   4E   5A   6J
    7I   8F   9G   10H

Unit 39

A 1 get out of
    2 get away
    3 getting on
    4 get in
    5 get by
    6 got out
    7 get over
    8 get round to
    9 get through
    10 get up
    11 get off
    12 get on with

B 1 got on well
    2 got away with
    3 get through to
    4 got over
    5 getting/growing old
    6 to get out of

C 1 off   4 out of
    2 through   5 over
    3 round

Unit 40

A 1 turn down
    2 turned up
    3 turned to
    4 turn back
    5 turned away
    6 turned out
    7 turn over
    8 turn off/out
    9 turned down
    10 turned against

11 turned into
12 turned on

B 1B 2C 3D 4A 5F 6H
7E 8G

C 1 off   4 down
2 over   5 out
3 to

Unit 41

A 1C 2L 3B 4K 5A 6D
7J 8H 9G 10I 11F
12E

B 1 will   9 was
2 always   10 doing
3 to   11 ✔
4 ✔   12 away
5 to   13 ✔
6 to   14 us/out
7 ✔   15 the
8 of   16 us

C 1B 2A 3D 4E 5C

Unit 42

A 1T 2F 3F 4T 5T 6F
7F 8T

B 1 b   4 a
2 a   5 c
3 d   6 d

C 1 forward to   4 come off
2 get   5 went
3 up   6 came

D 1D 2C 3B 4E 5A 6I
7J 8G 9F 10H

E 1 up
2 run
3 at
4 into
5 take

6 look
7 off
8 stands
9 to
10 across
11 seeing
12 going/getting/carrying

F 1B 2A 3C 4B 5D 6C
7A 8A 9D 10B

Unit 43

A 1 vacancies
2 applicants
3 post
4 application
5 curriculum vitae
6 employer
7 experience
8 Personnel Manager
9 interview
10 promotion
11 training
12 salary

B 1D 2E 3F 4C 5H 6B
7A 8G

C 1 resign
2 sack
3 pension
4 redundant, job
5 salary

Unit 44

A 1 compulsory   7 state
2 primary   8 private
3 secondary   9 fees
4 exams   10 boarding
5 marks   11 term
6 reports

B 1 education   6 subject
2 training   7 degree
3 career   8 grant
4 studies   9 graduate
5 university

Unit 45

A 1 planet
2 chemicals
3 ozone
4 rainforests
5 pollution
6 climate
7 ecological
8 resources
9 endangered species
10 die out
11 habitats
12 in captivity

B 1 conservation
2 fuel
3 energy sources
4 Recycle
5 bottle banks
6 public transport
7 exhaust fumes
8 greenhouse effect
9 Campaign
10 wildlife

Unit 46

A 1 trial   7 judge
2 evidence   8 verdict
3 witnesses   9 Guilty
4 jury   10 sentenced
5 court   11 prison
6 prisoner

B 1 hijacker   4 arsonist
2 kidnapper   5 shoplifter
3 pickpocket   6 burglar

C 1 solicitor
2 committing
3 charge
4 burglar
5 theft

Unit 47

A 1 immunized
2 infectious
3 treatment
4 incurable
5 conditions
6 cure
7 medical
8 symptoms
9 alternative medicine
10 homeopathy
11 Acupuncture

B 1 keep fit
2 exercise
3 jogging
4 Aerobics
5 giving up
6 overweight
7 go on a diet
8 weight
9 stress
10 relaxation

Unit 48

A 1 package holiday
2 accommodation
3 brochures
4 resort
5 bed and breakfast
6 self-catering
7 charter flight
8 passengers
9 check in
10 insurance

B 1 tent
2 villa
3 apartment
4 chalet
5 hotel
6 youth hostel

C 1 trip   4 excursion
2 cruise   5 tour
3 travel

Unit 49

A 1 laboratories
2 scientists
3 experiments
4 research
5 factories
6 mass production
7 vending machines
8 labour-saving
9 invention
10 microchip
11 progress
12 technology

B 1I   2G   3K   4H   5B   6F
7A   8L   9C   10D   11J
12E

Unit 50

A 1 vegetarian
2 vegan
3 restaurants
4 starter
5 main course
6 dessert
7 recipes
8 cookery books
9 ingredients
10 meal
11 cook
12 eat out
13 take-away

B 1 rice   5 chips
2 eggs   6 steak
3 beef   7 cream
4 bread   8 ice-cream

C 1 onion (not fruit)
2 orange (not a vegetable)
3 sheep (an animal, not meat)
4 fig (not a vegetable)
5 lemon (not dairy food)
6 jam (not made from flour)
7 flour (not used for flavouring)

8 tomato (a vegetable, not protein)
9 lemonade (not drunk hot or with milk)
10 milk (non alcoholic)

Unit 51

A 1 superstars
2 flying visit
3 ambition
4 hospitably
5 autographs
6 respect
7 privacy
8 publicity
9 popular

B 1 alone
2 opportunity
3 wealthy
4 retirement
5 second home
6 detached
7 hippies

Unit 52

A 1 go out with
2 fell in love
3 get married
4 fiancée
5 engaged
6 reception
7 honeymoon
8 wedding
9 bridegroom
10 best man
11 bride
12 bridesmaids

B 1 teenager
2 generation gap
3 argued
4 respected
5 jealous
6 broke off
7 relationship
8 drifted apart

Unit 53

A
1 recorded   6 tickets
2 audience   7 stage
3 broadcast   8 presenter
4 admission   9 rehearsal
5 press   10 applause

B
1 fun   5 performances
2 viewers   6 live
3 review   7 guest
4 season   8 great
   ticket   9 call for

Unit 54

A
1 account
2 pay in
3 cheque book
4 cash
5 credit card
6 purchases
7 current account
8 withdraw
9 overdraft
10 statement
11 deposit account
12 interest

B
1 note
2 currency
3 change, coins
4 exchange rate
5 mortgage
6 deposit
7 tax, income
8 cheque

Unit 55

A On the other hand, However, In addition, approximately, Furthermore, Therefore, Yours faithfully, I apologize, I intend to

B arrived, opened, have come/am coming, am taking/shall be taking, am going/shall be going, would like, to close, am writing, to ask, to transfer, have already given, will/would you send, showing, will/shall return, would like, to be closed, look forward to, receiving

Unit 56

A
1 I'm sorry I'm late.
2 We must have/find/get somewhere to stay.
3 Thank you for your help.
4 Have you decided yet?
5 I think you'll (probably) fail.
6 (Please) write (back) soon.
7 You've made a big mistake.

B
1 Never mind
2 Remember
3 By the way
4 Congratulations
5 What's the new office like
6 Any chance
7 If you like
8 or something
9 What do you think
10 let me know

Unit 57

A *Possible answers:*
1 The best way to learn a language
2 Pollution – a world problem
3 Pets as companions
4 Improving life in towns
5 Slaves to fashion

B excellent facilities,
Moreover,
I would like to recommend...,
In general,
Another disadvantage...,
In conclusion,
superb accommodation

Unit 58

A *Possible answers:*
1 Standing there was the man who had followed her home.
2 'How To Make a Million,' he read.
3 (Without even opening it,) she knew what it would say.
4 He was right.
5 It had been a very dangerous journey.
6 (After some hesitation,) I finally agreed to the contract.
7 The police arrived just in time.
8 Now she had nothing to worry about.

C
1B but
2D although
3F that
4C because
5A in order to
6E where

Unit 59

B 1A, D, E   2A, D, E   3B
4C   5B   6A, D, E

C
1 while
2 although
3 so far ... that
4 despite
5 as well as
6 in case
7 where

D
1 To start with
2 Furthermore/In addition
3 In addition/Furthermore
4 On the other hand
5 despite
6 To sum up
7 whereas

Test 1

A
1	b	11	d
2	a	12	c
3	c	13	a
4	b	14	b
5	a	15	c
6	d	16	d
7	c	17	d
8	b	18	c
9	a	19	a
10	b	20	b

B
1 in
2 have
3 a
4 body
5 not
6 who
7 an
8 about/approximately/over
9 ago/before
10 found/discovered
11 tall
12 known
13 Although
14 been
15 It
16 find/hunt/get
17 were
18 other
19 mystery
20 be

C
1 hadn't fallen, he would
2 should be put away by
3 had a table made by
4 prevented Andrew from getting
5 you needn't show
6 time I started
7 isn't as intelligent as
8 asked Nicola to open

D
1 look for
2 take off
3 taken on
4 look after
5 look through/over
6 look into/take up
7 takes after
8 take up
9 taken over
10 take in

Test 2

A 1A 2B 3D 4B 5A 6A
7C 8B 9D 10A 11D
12B 13C 14A 15C

B
1 was
2 little
3 life/education
4 that
5 began/started
6 and
7 In
8 a
9 whose
10 he
11 which
12 people
13 Their
14 most
15 in
16 For
17 but/although
18 made
19 where
20 at

C
1 has his clothes washed
2 I were you, I wouldn't
3 is being built by
4 dances better than
5 told me to get on
6 hasn't been fishing for
7 put Alan up
8 is (very) keen on

D
1 put out
2 putting, through
3 brought on
4 put in
5 brought up
6 bringing out
7 put off
8 putting down
9 brings in
10 brought about

Test 3

A
1	d	11	a
2	c	12	b
3	b	13	b
4	a	14	d
5	c	15	c
6	b	16	a
7	c	17	d
8	a	18	b
9	b	19	c
10	d	20	a

B
1 first/originally
2 in
3 however
4 be
5 damage
6 have
7 ever
8 chemicals/pollution
9 and
10 of
11 worse
12 in
13 levels/pollution
14 hoped/expected
15 as
16 reduce
17 use/production
18 no
19 is
20 cause

C
1 having the office redecorated
2 Betty was awarded first prize
3 if he had been wearing
4 in case anyone wants
5 in order to

6 doesn't eat as much

7 have had/owned their cottage for

8 looking forward to visiting

D 1E 2C 3D 4A 5B 6 H
7F 8J 9G 10I

Test 4

A 1D 2A 3B 4C 5A 6C
7A 8C 9D 10A 11C
12D 13A 14C 15D

B 1 one
2 has
3 buried/deep/lying/
4 in
5 years
6 documents/papers/writings/ books
7 famous/known/renowned
8 the
9 to
10 had
11 some
12 also
13 only/finally/eventually
14 when
15 took
16 desert/site
17 by
18 tracks/paths
19 important/ancient
20 be

C 1 the documents been received by
2 only he wouldn't/didn't
3 had her grass cut
4 like to come
5 the neighbours if you shout
6 might have left
7 in case the restaurant was
8 had been better

D 1 setting up
2 brought back
3 stand by
4 take down

5 stands for
6 bring, round
7 set off
8 take, away
9 bring up
10 stand in

Test 5

A 1 the   9 another
2 ✔   10 in
3 the   11 to
4 with   12 ✔
5 to   13 of
6 a   14 will
7 more   15 ✔
8 in   16 ✔

B 1 political
2 usual
3 better
4 economic
5 accurate
6 national
7 trained
8 less
9 surprised
10 categorically
11 disappointingly

C 1 for
2 as
3 to
4 animals
5 make/produce
6 houses/villages
7 have
8 which/that
9 nowadays/now/today
10 been
11 Most/Some
12 However
13 cheese
14 manner/style/fashion/way
15 soon
16 type/kind/sort
17 bans/forbids/prohibits

18 milk
19 that
20 come

D 1 have the chimney swept
2 if she comes
3 he was offered
4 don't cost as much
5 asked where she could find
6 despite the good
7 had always wanted to become
8 you needn't eat/don't need to eat/don't have to eat

E 1 came across
2 get by
3 get over
4 come off
5 get off
6 get away
7 come up
8 come up with
9 get out of
10 got away with
11 getting on
12 come round
13 come into
14 coming out
15 getting on

Test 6

A 1 c   11 c
2 c   12 b
3 b   13 a
4 a   14 b
5 b   15 c
6 c   16 d
7 a   17 a
8 b   18 c
9 d   19 c
10 d   20 b

B 1 best
2 became/was
3 wrote/produced
4 With
5 which

6 to
7 taught
8 many/most/several
9 history
10 in
11 information/knowledge
12 French/contemporary
13 also/even
14 the
15 whose
16 by
17 In
18 famous/known
19 of
20 innocent

C 1 apologized for forgetting
2 you mustn't park
3 in case I get
4 in spite of being
5 a few fans came
6 wished she had taken
7 was almost destroyed by
8 have the film developed

D 1 gone/going off
2 go with
3 turned up
4 gone out
5 turn, down
6 went down
7 turned, away
8 went on
9 turned, down
10 turn to

Test 7

A 1 got   10 ✔
2 the   11 ✔
3 by   12 an
4 ✔   13 for
5 to   14 she
6 sudden   15 often
7 ✔   16 of
8 has   17 ✔
9 was

B 1 generally   7 expensive
2 dangerous   8 solution
3 healthy   9 appreciate
4 economical 10 advice
5 distances   11 tourist
6 convenient

C 1 the   11 spent
2 history   12 when/after
3 married/met 13 known/seen
4 was   14 again
5 who   15 took
6 wedding   16 journey
7 Although   17 where
8 in   18 had
9 even   19 last
10 her   20 broken

D 1 such a good player that
2 objects to people asking
3 must have left
4 even though several players were
5 accused the boy of stealing
6 last went skiing
7 didn't/wouldn't let him play
8 succeeding in getting
9 earned more/were paid more

E 1C 2E 3A 4B 5 D 6G
7J 8F 9H 10I

Test 8

A 1 b   11 a
2 c   12 c
3 a   13 d
4 d   14 b
5 a   15 d
6 c   16 a
7 b   17 c
8 b   18 d
9 d   19 b
10 c   20 b

B 1 said/considered/reported
2 in
3 fell/was
4 win
5 in/over
6 For
7 but
8 returned
9 who
10 by
11 spent
12 where
13 lost
14 was
15 that
16 nothing
17 However
18 when
19 room(s)/palace
20 without

C 1 is very little water.
2 while she was talking to
3 offered to help the girl
4 never tasted such delicious
5 wasn't allowed (to have)
6 time he got
7 wished he hadn't refused/wished he had accepted
8 will be done

D 1 gets on
2 turn back
3 turn, into
4 give up
5 broke/got in
6 gave, away
7 broke up
8 get round to